Insights from EFFECTIVE CHURCHES *on*
New Member Classes and Assimilation

MEMBERSHIP
MATTERS

CHUCK LAWLESS

ZONDERVAN®

ZONDERVAN.com/
AUTHORTRACKER
follow your favorite authors

Membership Matters
Copyright © 2005 by Charles E. Lawless Jr.

Requests for information should be addressed to:
Zondervan, *Grand Rapids, Michigan 49530*

Library of Congress Cataloging-in-Publication Data

Lawless, Charles E., 1961–
    Membership matters : insights from effective churches on new member
classes and assimilation / Charles E. Lawless, Jr.—1st ed.
    Summary: "Based on a national study, this book shows how churches can
move both new and old members into ministry by implementing effective new
members' classes"—Provided by publisher.
       p. cm.
    Includes bibliographical references and index.
    ISBN-10: 0-310-26286-0 (jacketed hardcover)
    ISBN-13: 978-0-310-26286-2
    1. Church membership. 2. Church work with new church members.
3. Christian education of adults. 4. Lay ministry—Recruiting. I. Title.
BV820.L29   2005
254'.5—dc22   2005001129

Interior design by Michelle Espinoza

Printed in the United States of America

09 10 11 12 13 • 19 18 17 16 15 14 13 12 11 10 9 8 7 6 5 4

*To Dean Thom Rainer and my colleagues
at the Billy Graham School of Missions,
Evangelism and Church Growth;
and, as always, to Pam, the love of my life*

Contents

Illustrations

TABLES

FOREWORD

Thom Rainer

The American church is in crisis. I take no joy in being a bearer of bad news, and I understand that many may conclude I have embraced the attitude of Chicken Little and declared that the sky is falling. But no matter from what angle I view the realities of the American church, I see many ominous signs.

In congregations in the United States, only one person becomes a Christian for every eighty-five church members in a year's time. Our evangelistic harvests have dwindled to a point that they are hardly measurable.

Other researchers besides me have lamented the growth of doctrinal and biblical ignorance in our churches today. For the sake of brief illustration, I will cite just one indicator in this direction. Among *active* church members, nearly one out of six cannot name all of the four gospels of the New Testament. Matthew, Mark, Luke, and John are fast becoming names of obscurity to many of our members.

Perhaps a greater concern is that many evangelical church members are denying some of foundational truths of the Christian faith. Our most recent research found that one out of four evangelical church members do not fully subscribe to the exclusivity of salvation through Jesus Christ. John 14:6 is simply doubted or denied by many.

Does the crisis in the American church leave us without hope? Is it time to shake the dust off our feet and leave our churches to die a slow but certain death? Are our church buildings about to mirror the buildings of many churches in some European nations? Will we soon tour these empty edifices as museums and relics of the past?

Despite my gloomy assessments, I do hold on to the hope of recovery and revival in our churches. I do see signs of health and hope in the midst of seemingly sick and hopeless congregations.

One of the glimmers of hope comes from a man I have known for over a decade. Chuck Lawless and I have known each other in our relationship at the seminary where we work, in my consulting firm, and as friends. Dr. Lawless is also concerned about the health of the American church. But instead of bemoaning its demise, he has committed his life and ministry to doing something about it.

Chuck and I have seen many churches view their constituencies in one of two ways. One group of churches has minimal expectations of its members, if any expectations at all. Membership is meaningless in terms of commitment and accountability. These churches typically see significant fallout of members to inactivity. When membership does not matter, the members will care little about their levels of commitment. Another group of churches does not even encourage attenders to become members. For them, membership is an unbiblical concept that they refuse to impose on the local church. This group of churches also sees low levels of commitment among those who regularly attend.

But Chuck Lawless has discovered a number of churches that defy both of these descriptions. These churches and their leaders view membership as an expectation and a means of accountability. They are not as interested in a numerical count of names on a roll as in equating membership with belonging and responsibility. These churches tend to attract *and* assimilate persons effectively.

Dr. Lawless does not leave you with simply the theory of meaningful membership; to the contrary, you will see many vibrant churches and meet many church leaders applying these principles with great God-given success. And the greater news is that the application of many of these principles can be transferred to *your* churches.

I pray you will read this book with a sense of expectancy for what God will do when his people take his church seriously. I also pray you'll get several people in your church to read this book with you.

We live in a difficult age of cultural moral relativity and low congregational commitment—a combination proving deadly in many churches today. But we also serve a God of great hope, a God who promises to be with his people when they return to him.

Above all, *Membership Matters* is a book about the people of God returning to their first love. There are indeed many signs of hope. This book is a book of hope and possibility in difficult days. Read it for enjoyment. Read it for encouragement. But more than anything, read it to see what God might do in your church for his glory.

Thom Rainer is founding dean of the Billy Graham School of Missions, Evangelism and Church Growth at The Southern Baptist Theological Seminary in Louisville, Kentucky. He is the author of Surprising Insights from the Unchurched and Proven Ways to Reach Them *and* Breakout Churches.

ACKNOWLEDGMENTS

During the writing of this book, I celebrated my thirtieth anniversary as a Christian. It's hard to believe it was three decades ago that God drew me to himself and made me his child. Little did I know then that he would graciously give me opportunities to pastor two great churches, preach the Word on short-term mission trips, and now serve as a seminary professor. To him I say "thank you" again and again, not only for helping me complete the task of writing this book, but more so for giving me life. I am a man blessed far beyond what I deserve.

I will always be grateful to the members of Mt. Calvary Baptist Church in Harrison, Ohio, and Rolling Hills Baptist Church in Fairfield, Ohio, for giving me the privilege of serving as their pastor. In both churches, we wrestled with the question that drives this book: "How do we bring our guests into the congregation and then into ministry?" Though I'm sure we could have done things better, both of these churches allowed us to experiment until we had created some workable system. Thanks, folks, for taking a risk on a young pastor and being willing to change as needed.

My dean and friend Thom Rainer first encouraged me to study membership classes many years ago. Dr. Rainer is, in my opinion, without peer in the field of evangelism and church growth. I admit my bias (as he is also my boss), but no one is doing the research he's doing while calling the North American church to return to evangelistic church growth. Thank you, Dr. Rainer, for your friendship, as well as for your willingness to write the foreword to this book.

One of the joys of my ministry at Southern Seminary is the opportunity to work with students who have an incredible passion for the Lord. Two of those students led our research team for this project. The project began under the leadership of Brandon Conner, who has since graduated and entered his first pastorate in South Georgia (in a growing church that has a membership class). I consider Brandon a son, and I am excited to watch what the Lord is now doing through his own growing ministry. Thanks, Brandon, for your work on this project, your friendship with me, and your faithfulness to the Lord.

Matthew Spradlin oversaw the project to its conclusion. Matthew has an undeniable zeal for the Lord, for the Word, and for evangelism and church growth. I suspect this project is only the first of many on which you will see his name in years to come. Thanks, Matt, for keeping this project moving.

Other team members who contributed to our study were Jeff Pennington, Elisha Rimestad, John Dearing, Stuart Swicegood, and Travis Northcutt. Thanks to all of you for your efforts.

I cannot say enough about the great publishing team at Zondervan. Paul Engle, Dirk Buursma, Mike Cook, and the others have been the most thorough, encouraging team I've ever worked with. It has been my blessing to be associated with Zondervan for the second time.

And, as always, I must express my gratitude to my wife, Pam. Many were the weekends and evenings when she patiently found something else to do while I was finishing this book—but not once did she complain. God could not have given me a better spouse. Pam, I will always love you for your support, your prayers, and your gentle spirit.

And, to you, the reader, thank you for taking the time to read this book. I trust you will find it to be worthwhile reading.

Chapter 1

THE CHALLENGE

Moving Attenders into Membership and Ministry

Paul attended First Church every Sunday morning. In fact, he had joined the church and was one of the most consistent worship attenders in his congregation. Other church members often commented on how faithful Paul and his family were.

Yet, despite his perceived faithfulness, Paul wasn't involved in the church's ministry. He was gifted and talented, but Sunday morning worship attendance was his limit. Paul was what we call in this study an "uninvolved member."

Sitting across the aisle from Paul were the Staffords, a young couple seeking a church home. They enjoyed the worship at First, and their children were fitting in well in the Sunday school classes. In fact, they were just waiting for someone to explain to them the church's process for membership. While they waited, they remained only attenders.

Across town, three uninvolved believers sat faithfully in their own pews. Reba was a new member who really wanted to get involved in the church. She was waiting for someone to ask for her help, but no one did. John was a long-standing member who had decided several years ago that it was time "for the younger people to carry the load in the church." Sterling simply *attended* the church; actually *joining* wasn't in his plans.

On any given Sunday, uninvolved churchgoers sit in almost every congregation in America. In some cases, they are like the Staffords and Reba—ready and willing, just waiting for leaders to direct them and give them an opportunity.

Sometimes they are like Sterling. They are faithful to attend Sunday morning worship. They write a check each week to support the church. Ask them about their church, and they'll gladly tell you, "We go to such and such church." Yet, they never join.

In still other cases, they are like Paul and John. They have signed the membership rolls of the church. What they don't do, though, is *get involved*. Attendance does not lead to action. Church is more about *receiving* than giving, more about *coming* than going, and more about *being served* than serving.

The good news, however, is that these attenders and uninvolved members are *potential* sitting in a pew. That's one of the reasons our team wanted to do this study.

I assume you are a church leader who has faced some of these situations. You must want to move people into membership and ministry, because you've chosen to read this book. Whether you are trying to develop an effective membership process or simply trying to motivate those who remain uninvolved, this book is for you.

THE BACKGROUND OF THIS STUDY

For the last decade, our research teams at the Billy Graham School of Missions, Evangelism and Church Growth have been studying evangelistic churches in America. Two of these studies, led by Thom Rainer, indicated the significance of membership classes in growing churches.[1] This study began as a much more detailed look at these classes and, as you will see, then moved in a new direction.

CHURCH LEADERSHIP SURVEYS

There were three components to this research project. Our research team, which was led by Brandon Conner at the time, first sent a survey about membership classes to 150 growing churches (see appendix 14 for a copy of the survey). The questions addressed these kinds of topics:

- Does the church have a membership class? Is it required?
- Who teaches the class?
- What curriculum is used?
- What obstacles did the church face in starting a membership class?
- Who attends the class?

Seventy-one churches responded, with fifty-two (73 percent of those responding) indicating they had a membership class (table 1). The churches were primarily Southern Baptist, but four other groups were also represented in the survey responses: Presbyterian, Evangelical Free, Wesleyan, and independent community churches. The Sunday morning worship average attendances were fairly evenly distributed.

SIZE OF THE CHURCHES STUDIED		
Size of the church	Number of churches with a new member class (NMC)	Percentage of the total number of churches
Under 100	1	2
101 to 250	17	33
251 to 500	13	25
501 to 1,000	11	21
1,001 and up	10	19
TOTAL	52	100

Table 1

Twenty-one states were represented in the survey, including states from the South, the Midwest, the Northwest, the West, and the East Coast. In most cases, the membership class began under the leadership of the current pastor. All but three of the pastors were full-time, with an average tenure of 8.9 years at the church.

Table 2 lists the names used for the classes in these churches. Though certainly not original or creative, "new member class" was the name most frequently used.

NAME OF NEW MEMBER CLASS	
Class name	**Number of churches**
New Member Class	24
Discovering ____ Church/Class 101	16
Foundations	2
Basic Christian Education	1
Back to the Basics	1
More Than a Member	1
New Christian Study Group	1
RighTrack	1
Inquiry Class	1
Members on Mission	1
First Class	1
Welcome to the Family	1
Member Information Class	1

Table 2

CLASS MEMBER SURVEYS AND INTERVIEWS

In addition to surveying church leaders, our research team surveyed seventy-one laypersons who had attended membership classes at their churches (see appendix 15 for a copy of the survey). We asked questions like, "What did you find most beneficial about the class? Least beneficial? Do you believe a membership class should be required for all members? Are you still active in your church?"

These surveys gave us insights the leadership survey didn't give. In fact, as you will see, sometimes the leaders and class members had different opinions about the classes.

Research team leader Matthew Spradlin sought to get more information from the class members by personally contacting many of them via telephone or email. Their opinions about the classes were fascinating. As an example, consider the words of Deanna, who was a Christian for thirty-four years before she ever attended a membership class: "As a thirteen-year-old [when she became a Christian], I never attended a new member class. . . . [Now, having taken the class] I enjoyed and appreciated the class. I think the new member class should be offered and available for everyone—as new members or as a refresher course for any length of time as a Christian. Taking part in this class helps a person feel more like a member or a part of the local church."

You will see that other laypersons had similar opinions. In fact, all seventy-one class members we surveyed said that potential and current members should attend membership classes.

AN ADDITIONAL DIRECTION

In the course of our study, we heard this question over and over again: "We've got a membership class, but we struggle overall with getting other members involved. What do we do about the current members who aren't doing ministry?" Other pastors who had heard about our study also told us about faithful attenders who simply never joined. So often did we hear these concerns that we knew this study needed to take an additional turn.

Our research team then more specifically investigated how growing churches move attenders into membership and ministry. In some cases, these churches were the same ones that participated in the new members study. We included other churches, though, simply because we discovered they had developed workable systems for leading their congregations to get involved.

Our researchers began to survey pastors, review programs, and interview formerly uninvolved members who decided to move from the pew into ministry. You will read about these findings throughout this book.

A FEW SURPRISES

Every research team must admit—if it's honest—that it begins the study expecting to discover certain things. In fact, *bias* might be the better term. Our research team was no different. Many of our assumptions were proven correct (for example, we assumed that the pastor's role in a membership class is significant). Some findings, though, surprised us. Perhaps giving you a taste of the results will whet your appetite to read on.

OPPOSITION TO REQUIRED NEW MEMBER CLASSES SEEMS TO BE DECREASING

Thom Rainer's 1997 study of church assimilation showed that 72.7 percent of the churches studied either required or expected new members to attend membership classes.[2] Our study revealed almost identical numbers: 73.2 percent of the churches responding to our survey utilized membership classes.

An intriguing shift is apparent, though. The percentage of churches that *require* members to attend membership classes increased from 18.2 percent in the 1997 study to 31.0 percent of the churches in this study. Correspondingly, the percentage of churches that *expected but did not require* attendance at membership classes decreased from 54.5 percent to 39.4 percent. Take a look at the shifts (figure 1).

Throughout every component of this study, we saw this trend: more churches are now *requiring* attendance at a membership class. The Rainer study found that church leaders often faced significant opposition to requiring membership classes, but our study found remarkably little opposition. Indeed, only five of the twenty-two churches with required membership classes indicated any opposition to the change.

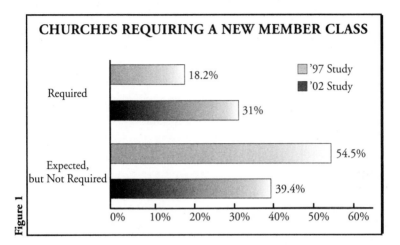

CHURCHES REQUIRING A NEW MEMBER CLASS

'97 Study
'02 Study

Required — 18.2%
31%

Expected, but Not Required — 54.5%
39.4%

0% 10% 20% 30% 40% 50% 60%

Figure 1

RELATIONSHIPS REALLY DO MATTER

In the first part of our study, church leaders were asked to indicate the primary purpose or purposes of their membership classes. Take a moment to think about this question, and try to guess what the results showed us (figure 2).

It is probably not surprising to you that leaders viewed the primary purposes as providing church orientation (average score on a scale of 1 to 5: 4.59), followed closely by teaching doctrine (4.25). Using the class to introduce new members to each other (3.48) and to the church staff ranked the lowest of the options (3.05). From the perspective of these church leaders, the membership class was more about information than relationships.

Class members, however, told us something slightly different in their survey. Using a scale of 1 to 10 (1 = strongly disagree, 5 = uncertain, and 10 = strongly agree), they responded to fifteen statements designed to evaluate how class participation influenced their lives. Notice the top responses:

PURPOSES OF A NEW MEMBER CLASS

Using a scale of 1 to 5, 1 being not at all a purpose, 3 being somewhat a purpose, and 5 being a primary purpose, indicate the purpose(s) of your new member class.

_____ a. providing orientation to the church in general

_____ b. teaching about the church's basic doctrine

_____ c. building relationships among new members

_____ d. introducing class members to the church staff

_____ e. offering opportunities for new members to get involved in the ministry of the church

_____ f. carrying out evangelism—sharing the gospel with class members

_____ g. other: _____

_____

Figure 2

- I now know the church's expectations for its members (score: 9.07).
- I know more about my church now (8.39).
- I am more willing to invite friends to church now (8.29).
- I would be more comfortable talking to my pastor now (8.28).
- I know more people in the church now (8.12).

Not surprisingly, these laypersons indicated that, above everything else, they gained knowledge of the church and its expectations. The next three highest scores, though, point to the relational benefits of membership classes. This focus becomes more apparent when we see that the five *lowest* responses to this question were related to spiritual disciplines or doctrinal knowledge, including "I know more about God now" (6.87). Clearly, relationships were important to new members.

Our study also showed us that relationships established in membership classes can be used effectively to motivate even un-involved members to get involved in ministry. There is more on this finding in chapter 3.

EXPECTATIONS YES, CHURCH DISCIPLINE NO

Thom Rainer's book *High Expectations* showed that growing churches tend to have high standards for members. So it didn't surprise us that in their new member classes, 96 percent of the churches emphasized membership expectations. Nor were we caught off guard by statements like these from class members:

- It [the class] helped us understand what the church wants.
- It was really good because it told us what's expected of us as members.

What *did* surprise us, though, was this finding: while 96 percent of the churches emphasized expectations, only 25 percent addressed church discipline in their membership classes. That is, churches raised the bar of membership but failed to talk about what would happen if church members didn't live up to those expectations.

We will analyze this discrepancy more in chapter 5. For now, however, understand that many of these churches were still work-ing through the details and implications of having membership classes. On average, these classes had existed for five years, yet 80 percent of the survey respondents said they wanted to get their hands on *any* information we discovered in order to strengthen their classes.

Because many of these churches are continually developing their classes, they had by no means always resolved all of the issues involved. How to address church discipline in a membership class—and then, how to implement it when expectations are not met—seemed to be an unresolved issue. Again, we'll return to this topic in chapter 5.

WHAT ABOUT EVANGELISM IN A MEMBERSHIP CLASS?

Matthew Spradlin, one of the lead researchers on this project, spent many hours analyzing data, crunching numbers, interviewing staff members and laypersons, and offering his own conclusions to this research. In particular, one summary conclusion surprised me: "Usually when we think of new member classes [NMC], we think of assimilation, of incorporating new believers into the church. We don't typically think of evangelism. But the NMC can be used as a powerful tool of evangelism. There were several churches in the study that used their NMC as a way to reach the lost with the gospel. This study has shown me that, if done evangelistically, a membership class can be an effective tool for leading persons to Jesus."

Matthew's summary is right on target. Some of the names used for these classes don't imply evangelism (e.g., New Member Class, New Member Orientation, Members on Mission), but 43 percent of the churches said that evangelism was "a primary purpose" of their classes. Indeed, they ranked this purpose as a 5 on a scale of 1 to 5. Chapter 4 will give more details about this significant issue.

NOT EVERY CHURCH STRUGGLES WITH ATTENDERS WHO DO NOT JOIN

In the course of our research, our team asked pastors to respond to the concern that people do not want to join churches today. While enough leaders recognized this issue that we've addressed it in chapter 6, Pastor Douglas New of Mt. Pleasant Baptist Church in Carrollton, Georgia, expressed our overall findings: "I disagree with that statement. . . . People like to belong if it really means something."

Indeed, when we asked these leaders about their plan for addressing attenders who never join, few could articulate an intentional strategy. Sometimes the response was momentary silence as leaders were forced to think about many attenders who had *not* joined.

Remember, we chose the churches in our original survey because they were already reaching people for Christ; attenders *were*, in fact, joining their churches. Seldom did they face the attender membership problem to the extent other pastors did. To prove that point, the churches with membership classes in our study averaged *106* additions during the year of our study!

Chapter 6 will look at what these churches and others did to encourage membership. They have much to teach churches that are trying hard to get attenders to join.

EVEN LONG-STANDING UNINVOLVED MEMBERS CAN BE MOTIVATED TO SERVE

I hear it all the time from my seminary students: "Dr. Lawless, I've decided to plant a church. That way, I can start from scratch, and I won't have to deal with members who aren't interested in doing anything." There *are* advantages to starting from scratch in church planting, but this study has shown that even long-standing uninvolved members can be moved into ministry.

Paul was one of those members (remember his story at the beginning of this chapter?). His pastor began to seek ways to motivate uninvolved members, and one simple change in the church's recruitment process made a difference for Paul.

For years, a nominating committee of three members had the responsibility of enlisting workers at Paul's church. The committee members were chosen simply because they knew many church members—not because they had a passion for the ministries for which they sought workers. The problem is, dispassionate recruiters usually give up easily and settle for anyone when workers are hard to find.

The new process allowed Paul's pastor and the committee to recommend primary ministry leaders, who were then authorized to enlist other workers for their ministries. The nominating committee's work was essentially done when the ministry leaders were selected. In this approach, the recruiters were those whose enthusiasm for particular ministries was hard to rebuff.

A zealous men's ministry leader—who, like Paul, once thought he didn't have any more time to give to the church—convinced Paul to get involved. A passionate recruiter and a new process made the difference for this once uninvolved church member.

Paul's story is only one of several you will hear throughout this book.

THE DIRECTION OF THIS BOOK

This chapter has been introductory, designed to give a general summary of the study. Chapter 2 tackles the scheduling issue: How did these churches fit membership classes into already busy schedules? In the context of this chapter, I also propose one reason why so many church members continue to just sit in the pews.

Chapter 3 examines the importance of relationships in a membership class, including a look at how such a class can motivate other members to get involved in ministry. If you are a pastor, you'll especially want to read this chapter.

Chapters 4 and 5 address the challenge church leaders most commonly voiced: How can we find good curriculum for membership classes? In these chapters, we describe the content of the classes we studied, while directing you to helpful resources as well. You'll find interesting examples both there and in the recommended appendixes.

Chapter 6 specifically asks the question "How do we get people to join and to do ministry in the first place?" In some ways, the rest of the book answers this question. Churches that make membership matter simply *expect* people to join and to get to work. Nevertheless, chapter 6 provides particular insights into this issue.

Chapter 7 is a how-to chapter to help you start making membership matter in your church. Several simple guidelines will point you and your church in the right direction. We'll also deal with two other questions raised during our study:

- What do we do about older members who have never attended a membership class?
- Should there be different classes for new believers and for transferred church members?

Several leaders of growing churches contributed significantly to chapter 8. Here you will find their churches' specific stories of how they make membership matter. All of these leaders have insights I think you'll find helpful, if not stretching.

A brief closing chapter offers a final challenge for churches that want to move attenders into membership and ministry. We trust you will accept the challenge.

At the end of nearly every chapter are sections called "Helpful Appendixes" and "Questions for Consideration." The appendixes, we believe, are among the most valuable components of this book. Don't ignore these, because you'll find there many samples of materials used by the churches studied. A list of all the churches that participated in any part of our study is included there as well. The questions are provided to help you reflect, both personally and with your fellow leaders, on the important issues of membership and assimilation in your particular church setting.

Finally, be sure to read the endnotes at the back of the book. There you will find other resources to help you make membership matter in your church.

FOR YOU

Not all of the churches that responded to our original survey offered membership classes. One Missouri pastor whose church did not have a class placed a Post-it note on his survey: "Thank you for this timely survey. I just came to this church and see a definite need for a new member class. I would be interested in any material you may have."

To this pastor I say, "This book is written for pastors and church leaders like you." Because other pastors told us they wanted help in motivating uninvolved attenders and members, we expanded the research to help them as well.

Our team has been, and still is, praying that God will use this study to help churches empower people—including attenders, new members, and long-standing members—to serve in their church. Thank you, reader, for allowing us to share our research with you. I trust you will be grateful you decided to read on.

HELPFUL APPENDIXES

Appendix 14: Church Survey
Appendix 15: New Member Survey

QUESTIONS FOR CONSIDERATION

1. What issues in your church are leading you to read this book?
2. What do you hope to learn from this book?
3. What percentage of attenders in your church have not joined the church?
4. What percentage of your church members are not currently serving in some ministry capacity?

Chapter 2

"Who's Got Time for Another Meeting?"

The Scheduling Issues

———⚮———

I was surprised by how strongly the California pastor spoke to his congregation of 250:

> We'll need more child care workers over the next few weeks as we prepare for Easter. Now, some of you may be thinking you need a break from your kids. Others of you are thinking you've already raised your children and shouldn't be asked to serve in the preschool department. Some of you just want to sit and enjoy the Easter services. But remember that when you signed on as a member of this church, you signed on to work, and if you aren't willing to help, you break your membership vows to this congregation.

It was that last sentence that caught my attention: *If you aren't willing to help, you break your membership vows to this congregation.* In this church, leaders emphasize a required membership class where prospective members learn that "uninvolved member" is a contradiction in terms. The church makes time to teach and train new members, and new members are then expected to make time to do ministry.

This chapter begins where our research project began—with membership classes. We'll find out that the churches we studied made these classes a priority. We'll conclude the chapter by examining the relationship between membership classes and membership involvement in general.

THE PRIORITY OF TRAINING NEW MEMBERS

Simply stated, the churches we studied made time for membership classes because they believed in their importance. Listen to what one pastor from the South told us:

> For years, I was frustrated because my church members really didn't know what we believed and didn't understand my vision. Somehow we just weren't connecting, so I started looking for another church. When God didn't open any other options, I knew I had to find a solution.
>
> The new member class was an answer to prayer. There I could teach doctrine and vision to all of our new members, so they could get on board as they joined. It wasn't easy getting the church to buy in to a required class, but I now wish I had started the class years earlier.

Our research indicates at least two reasons why these leaders believe membership classes are important. First, strong church membership begins with the *front door process*. People tend to be much more committed if the church publicly expects them to be committed up front—and a membership class provides a place to communicate these expectations.

Tiffany, a layperson from Lansing, Michigan, told one of our researchers, "You don't sign a contract without reading the fine print. Why join a church unless you know exactly what they believe and what they expect of you?" Not surprisingly, only one of the laypersons we interviewed hadn't yet become involved in the church several years after attending a membership class.

Second, a membership class is an opportunity to say, "What we believe and do is important." In my book *Discipled Warriors*, I argue that a healthy church produces disciples whose theological foundation is sound and whose faith influences all that they do.[3] The churches we studied told us that a membership class is the place to start this process. "Teach members early," one pastor told us, "and you can lay the foundation for a committed church membership. Don't apologize for who you are—just teach them."

The churches in our study used their membership classes to emphasize concisely and clearly what matters to the church. Consequently, fifty-one of the fifty-two churches surveyed asserted that their churches are stronger because of their membership classes, and the same high number told us that the work of planning and executing classes is well worth the effort.

In turn, one Texas lay leader told us after attending his church's membership class, "I know what's important to our church now, and I am very proud to say this is my church." He learned that membership really does mean something in his church, and he committed himself to be a faithful and serving member. This, we believe, is the way it ought to work.

THE DIFFICULTIES OF SCHEDULING A MEMBERSHIP CLASS

Back in 1981, I was pastoring a small church in southwestern Ohio. As the church grew, we knew we needed a class for new members. Recognizing the need, however, was the easy step; the difficult step was figuring out when to offer the class. We tried three different schedules before we settled on a four-week class that met for one hour each Sunday.

In this study, our research team heard about this same kind of scheduling dilemma. Generally, the issues revolved around two concerns: (1) How do we offer a workable schedule so that the greatest number can attend? and (2) How do we offer a schedule that allows us to cover the greatest amount of necessary material? As you might imagine, meeting both of these goals was not always easy.

WHEN DO THE CLASSES MEET?

Have you noticed how often the apostle Paul went to the synagogue when he first entered a city? He "proclaimed the word of God in the Jewish synagogues" in Salamis (Acts 13:5), in Pisidian Antioch (13:14), in Iconium (14:1), in Thessalonica (17:1), in Corinth (18:4), and in Ephesus (19:8). Paul went to the synagogue first because *that's where the people were*. The apostle sought to preach truth to religious people who had already gathered for instruction.

Our research team found the same general pattern among churches with membership classes. Forty-three out of fifty-two churches (82.7 percent) indicated that their class met on Sunday, the day when members were already accustomed to gathering. The length and time of the classes varied, but Sunday was clearly the day of choice (figure 3).

Several reasons were given for offering the class on Sunday. Obviously, the primary reason was that members were already coming to church that day. The busy schedules of senior pastors and staff members also necessitated selecting Sunday. Offering the class on Sunday was the most convenient for everyone involved, making it easier for more new members to attend and more staff members to participate.

Another reason for teaching the membership class during a regular Sunday schedule was a practical one: child care was readily available. If the class was offered during an established small group time, preschool care and children's education programs would typically be offered at the same time. Thus, twenty-two out of the fifty-two churches who had membership classes scheduled their

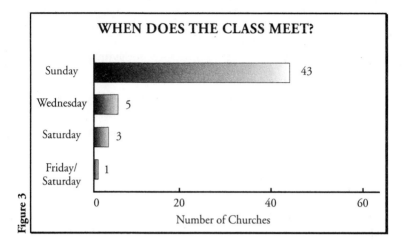

WHEN DOES THE CLASS MEET?

Figure 3

classes during a regular Sunday morning activity such as Sunday school.

Chapel Hill Presbyterian Church in Gig Harbor, Washington, offers one of the most unique schedules we encountered. Its class, called "Welcome to the Family," takes place over a weekend. Experience has taught that a brief but concentrated course best meets its needs; hence, the class meets Friday night (7:00–9:45 p.m.), all day Saturday (9:00 a.m.–5:00 p.m.), and Sunday for worship. The church provides all meals and child care.

The best time for us is late Sunday afternoon, as long as we provide both child care and a meal. There are very few things that conflict with the time, and we get the best turnout.

Bob Harrington, pastor of Harpeth Community Church, Franklin, Tennessee

If you're tempted to think this time commitment in one weekend is heavy, listen to how executive pastor Stuart Bond promotes the class in this portion of his invitation letter:

Dear friend,

I am so glad that you are interested in the upcoming Welcome to the Family class. Nearly a thousand people have come through this class in the past eight years. After every class, people have told me that this has been one of the most uplifting and inspiring experiences they have ever known. It is my prayer that you will clear your schedule and join us for this class, because I believe this will be just such an experience for you.

Among the benefits of this class are:

- Getting to know others in this church in a unique and powerful way. In one short weekend Chapel Hill will be changed for you from that "big" church you attend to a place where you worship with people you know.
- Getting to know the pastors more personally. We look forward to the opportunity to know you personally, and we commit significant time to each weekend.
- Understanding more about Chapel Hill's values and views on matters of faith.
- Having a chance to clarify your own faith story at this time in your life.
- Enjoying a weekend that is both relaxed and invigorating, one you will be sorry to see end.

Can you understand why almost a thousand people have attended these classes? I live a *long* way from Gig Harbor, but I'm almost ready to clear my calendar for the next membership class! Pastor Bond will tell more of this church's story in chapter 8.

How Long Are the Classes?

Several years ago, I was leading a discussion about church membership classes with a group of pastors. We reviewed a Billy Graham School study indicating that most classes were only several hours long on a single day, yet they covered more topics than seemed feasible in a short amount of time.[4]

"That's impossible," said one pastor. "How can you cover all of that in a few hours?" "I suspect it's just a quick review," said another. In the end, our group remained perplexed as to how these churches were accomplishing all they said they achieved.

I admit I hoped our study would show that churches were devoting more time to membership classes. On average, that was the case, though not decidedly so. The classes in our study averaged a total of five and a half hours in length. The shortest class met for only an hour and a half, and the longest class met for a total of sixteen hours (one hour each week for sixteen weeks). Figure 4 shows, however, that several churches were offering classes considerably longer than the average five and a half hours.

We did discover one decided difference from the previous study. Whereas 70 percent of the churches previously studied held a one-day membership class, 57 percent of the classes we surveyed met in multiple sessions over a series of weeks. Twenty-six of those classes met for at least four weeks. Our research team believes that multiple sessions helped create stronger relationships, as you will see in the next chapter.

As we analyzed the time frame for the class, a simple pattern became apparent: the number of class hours was often indicative of the primary purpose for the class. While our categorizations may be too simple, we have characterized these classes as either *informational* or *instructional*. Informational classes were designed largely to be an orientation to the church. Instructional classes, on the other hand, provided both orientation and some basic training in Christian disciplines (table 3).

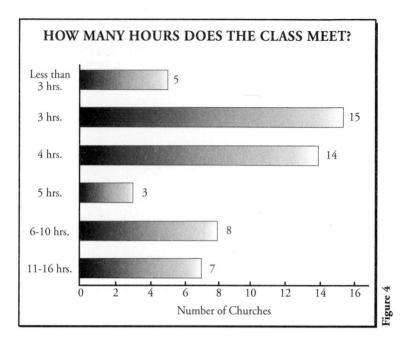

HOW MANY HOURS DOES THE CLASS MEET?

Less than 3 hrs. — 5

3 hrs. — 15

4 hrs. — 14

5 hrs. — 3

6-10 hrs. — 8

11-16 hrs. — 7

Number of Churches

Figure 4

Sandia Presbyterian Church in Albuquerque, New Mexico, offers an informational class that meets for three hours one Sunday a month. As you'll learn in chapter 8, this church encourages newcomers to get involved even before joining, and this "Inquiry Class" serves as the membership class. Pastor Dewey Johnson told us, "The purpose is to give basic information about the congregation so they can better participate if they so desire." Based on the content taught and the class length, 50 percent of the churches we studied offered a similar informational class rather than an instructional one.

HOW OFTEN ARE THE CLASSES OFFERED?

The frequency with which membership classes were offered varied considerably in the churches we studied (figure 5). For example, Faith Evangelical Church in Woodruff, Wisconsin, offers a class

INFORMATIONAL OR INSTRUCTIONAL CLASSES?	
Informational Class	**Instructional Class**
shorter time required	longer time required
offered more often each year	by necessity, offered less often
likely to be taught by the pastor	more likely to be taught by the pastor and others
more focused on general information about the church	stronger focus on church information, doctrinal teaching, and spiritual disciplines
emphasizes the "what" (What is the church about? What is its mission? What is its history? etc.)	emphasizes the "what" and the "how" (What is the church's mission? What are spiritual disciplines, and how do I do them?)
more likely to have guests attending who are "checking out" the church	guests attend, but more likely to have primarily new members attending
relationships important but developed and strengthened in other settings	relationships developed within the class setting; mentoring relationship sometimes established
evangelizing class members often a priority	evangelizing class members and teaching them to evangelize others more often a priority

Table 3

39

that meets for three consecutive Sundays during the Sunday school hour—but only once a year. The pastor meets individually with those new members who miss the scheduled class, but the class itself takes place annually.

At the other extreme is Mililani Baptist Church in Mililani, Hawaii. Mililani provides a four-session class that meets on consecutive Sunday evenings (5:45 p.m.–6:45 p.m.), with a new rotation of classes beginning every four weeks. Essentially, the membership class is offered continuously.

Faith Evangelical and Mililani Baptist were the exceptions rather than the norms in our study. As you might assume, informational classes were scheduled more often than instructional ones over the course of a year.

In the midst of this study, our research team uncovered one interesting fact regarding the frequency of class offerings. One way to evaluate a church's evangelistic outreach is to analyze the "baptismal ratio," calculated by dividing the number of resident members by the number of annual baptisms. In our study, churches that offered their classes more frequently (weekly or monthly) had a baptismal ratio of 1:11—that is, they baptized one person for every eleven members. The ratio for those that offered courses less frequently (1–3 times per year) was 1:15.

Both ratios are excellent, and we cannot draw dogmatic conclusions about this slight difference. Nevertheless, our anecdotal evidence suggests that churches with more frequent class offerings more consistently kept outreach in front of their congregations.

The result was circular. A continual outreach focus led to new members, which led to promoting membership classes offered more often. In those classes, leaders promoted outreach again by sharing the gospel and encouraging others to do the same. More membership classes then were needed as more outreach produced fruit.

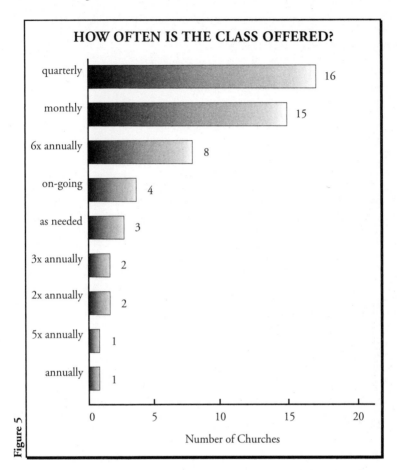

HOW OFTEN IS THE CLASS OFFERED?

Figure 5

THE CHALLENGE

The challenge for your church is to determine what schedule works best for you. Classes with fewer sessions tend to have more consistent attendance, but longer classes address more material. Whatever your decision is, catch the point: make your membership class a priority.

Uninvolved Members and Membership Classes: A Significant Relationship?

The Barna Research Group tells us that only 36 percent of born-again believers are likely to volunteer their time to help at a church.[5] That being the case, why do so many church members remain uninvolved? And how could a membership class help resolve this problem?

Will Langford did a study of uninvolved members when he was the pastor of Lakota Hills Baptist Church in West Chester, Ohio. Pastor Langford assumed correctly that many of his uninvolved members perceived they didn't have time to do ministry in the church. To his surprise, though, he learned that 68 percent remained uninvolved simply because they had "never been asked."[6]

Over the course of three months, Pastor Langford taught a Bible study about involvement, preached about the nature of the church, and deliberately used every possible opportunity to point out ministry needs in the church. It was then that he *intentionally asked* these uninvolved members to get involved.

What do you think the results were? Sixty-eight percent had said they were uninvolved because no one had asked them to serve; in the end, 69 percent actually began serving after their pastor asked them to do so! Pastor Langford made this observation:

> In years past, I have felt that asking for a commitment would drive people away from the church.... I learned that my previous assumption about church members' commitment was not correct. Many of the people I worked with ... were not afraid of commitment. There were some who desired to serve and were actually waiting for the opportunity to become involved in the ministry of the church.[7]

When we asked active laypersons in our study why they *were* involved in ministry, 56 percent indicated that someone had specifically asked them. The point is plain: asking someone to serve is a first step toward involvement, and some uninvolved members are just waiting for someone to ask.

What, then, is the connection with a membership class? Pastors in our study told us that members are often most excited—and most open to learning and getting involved in the church—*when they first join.*

In fact, take note of some general comments we heard during our project:

- New members are "keyed up" about the church; they want to get involved.
- New members are frequently looking for something to do, but they don't always know *how* to get involved.
- New members are usually willing to do what the church needs, *if* the church provides support.
- New members are especially ready to follow the pastor's lead. They respond positively to his asking them to serve.
- Some of our new members are the most excited people we have in the church.

Overall, our research team members noticed an undeniable excitement when laypersons or church leaders spoke about new members and membership classes. Passionate church leaders taught excited new members in the class, and that excitement fed the fervor of the leaders. In essence, an effective membership class throws fuel on a fire that is already burning well (figure 6).

Yet I can still hear some readers asking, "But what does this finding have to do with uninvolved members?" Simply this: an effective membership class is one step toward keeping members from becoming complacent and uninvolved in the first place. Ask new members to serve while their "fire" is still hot, and *prevention* then becomes the best cure for a lack of involvement.

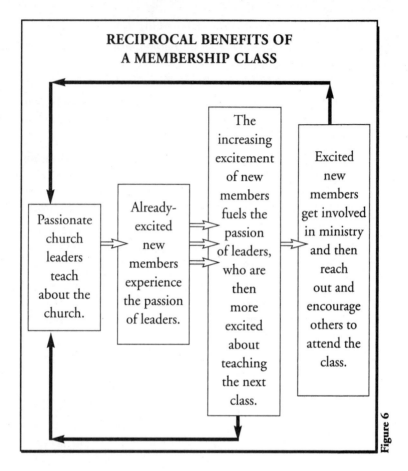

**RECIPROCAL BENEFITS OF
A MEMBERSHIP CLASS**

Passionate church leaders teach about the church.

Already-excited new members experience the passion of leaders.

The increasing excitement of new members fuels the passion of leaders, who are then more excited about teaching the next class.

Excited new members get involved in ministry and then reach out and encourage others to attend the class.

Figure 6

I know this truth well, for it's my own story. I became a Christian at the age of thirteen, and my associate pastor immediately asked me to help in the Sunday school bus ministry. One week after my baptism, I was visiting in the neighborhoods, inviting children and their parents to our church. I was not equipped to evangelize at the time, nor did I know much about the church. All I knew was that my associate pastor wanted me to help. Church involvement eventually became just a part of who I am.

Not everyone is so blessed to become assimilated into the church immediately. In fact, Charles Arn's research has shown that over 80 percent of the people who leave a church do so within the first six months of their membership.[8] Members who have few relationships and responsibilities in the church find little reason to stay—and the window of opportunity for getting them involved closes quickly.

In contrast, churches that emphasize membership and ministry through membership classes are much more likely to see attenders join and get to work. As we'll see throughout this book, membership classes build relationships and promote ministry opportunities. These churches, simply because they use membership classes well, do not miss the window of opportunity for assimilation.

Churches that choose *not* to make these classes a priority, however, may be unintentionally inviting attenders and members alike to remain uninvolved. For that reason alone, making time to schedule membership classes is imperative.

Some Enthusiastic Leaders

I recently led a conference attended by pastors and staff members of growing churches. When I asked participants to list the benefits of membership classes, their answers came quickly and enthusiastically.

"I get to know my new members personally," said one pastor. "Our new members get grounded in our major beliefs," said another. One staff member commented, "Our members now feel a part of the family." Still another said with great passion, "Our class has generated an enthusiasm and anticipation among new members that we've never seen before." He added, "We've greatly reduced the numbers dropping out or going out the back door. Members are getting involved."

Scheduling a membership class is never easy. Church staff members and potential class members are already too busy. Church calendars are already too full. But the leaders in this study told us that the benefits of the class far outweigh the scheduling difficulties. These churches simply *made it work* in the midst of hectic schedules.

HELPFUL APPENDIXES

Appendix 1: Sample Invitation Letter

QUESTIONS FOR CONSIDERATION

1. If your church doesn't have a membership class, what scheduling issues do you think you may encounter in implementing one? If you have such a class, what scheduling difficulties are you facing?
2. Is your current class (or planned one) more informational or instructional? What are your reasons for choosing this approach to the class?
3. In your estimation, what percentage of your church members are uninvolved simply because no one has specifically asked them to serve?
4. After reading this chapter, what one change or improvement might you make in your church's membership class?

Chapter 3

"What Matters Most to Me?"

The Relationship Issues

———— ⌇⌇ ————

I met "Butch" Ikels at a church growth conference in the fall of 2003. Butch, the pastor of the Country Church in Marion, Texas, beamed with excitement as he told me what God was doing in the church. From 1998 to 2003, the worship attendance average had increased from nine people meeting in a living room to 840 meeting in the Country Church building. In those five years, the church also started four other churches. The pastor preaches in boots and jeans, "no ties allowed—and guns must be checked at the door!"

I left that conversation thinking, "I suspect it's fun to go to his church. I'd like to talk to him some more."

Six times a year, a group of new members at the Country Church gets that opportunity. Pastor Butch personally invites new members and converts to attend a class that covers such topics as salvation, baptism, evangelism, the devotional life, giving, and spiritual gifts.

The pastor told our research team that the membership class is "one of the most fruitful ministries" of his pastorate. He observed,

"Over the eight weeks of the course, I get to really know approximately thirty new members." Those relationships then help Butch cast a shared vision for the church.

As you will find out in this chapter, relationships like these really do matter—both in reaching new members *and* in motivating uninvolved members.

RELATIONSHIPS AND CHURCH GROWTH

Several studies have shown that between 65 and 90 percent of laypersons first come to church through the witness of a relationship.[9] Maybe your Christian testimony is like mine and so many others—a story of relationships.

My younger brother was the first in our family to hear about salvation when a caring neighbor told him about Jesus. A seventh-grade classmate told me the good news. A brave Sunday school director asked me to teach my first Sunday school class. My wife was raised by Christian parents who guided her to hear and respond to Jesus. (Actually, my wife and I were introduced by two church secretaries who made it their business to facilitate relationships!) Clearly, relational connections are critical to leading others to Jesus Christ and his church.

More relevant to this study is the role of relationships in *keeping and motivating* church members. As figure 7 shows, our studies at the Billy Graham School have revealed four components of effective assimilation:[10]

- *Membership expectations* stated up front indicate the significance of church membership and weed out potential members who choose not to meet the expectations.
- *Ministry involvement* gives members purpose and responsibility in the church.
- *Convictional preaching* offers a message worth hearing—and a reason for staying involved.

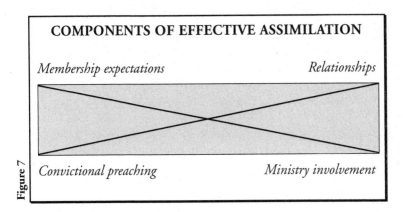

Figure 7

COMPONENTS OF EFFECTIVE ASSIMILATION

Membership expectations   *Relationships*

Convictional preaching   *Ministry involvement*

- *Relationships* create "people connections" that strengthen a member's commitment to the local body of believers.

These "people connections" are pivotal to reaching people and to keeping them. As one writer has stated, "Newcomers don't come with Velcro already applied. It's up to the congregation to make them stick."[11] Relationships are a major part of the Velcro.

Vern, a Midwestern layperson who participated in our study, understands this reality. A coworker first told Vern about Christ and invited him to attend his church, where Vern and his wife responded to the gospel in the church's membership class. Today, they are serving as ministry leaders in their church. They are evangelizing and discipling others, primarily through relationships.

Relationships in Membership Classes

As mentioned in chapter 1, our survey asked church leaders to describe the primary purpose or purposes of their membership classes. Figure 8 reveals the findings, with the average response noted in italics.

Unquestionably, church leaders intended orientation and doctrinal training to be the primary purposes of the class. Providing opportunities to meet other members and church staff members

PURPOSES OF A NEW MEMBER CLASS: FINDINGS

Using a scale of 1 to 5, 1 being not at all a purpose, 3 being somewhat a purpose, and 5 being a primary purpose, indicate the purpose(s) of your new member class.

_4.59_ a. providing orientation to the church in general

_4.25_ b. teaching about the church's basic doctrine

_3.86_ c. offering opportunities for new members to get involved in the ministry of the church

_3.78_ d. carrying out evangelism—sharing the gospel with class members

_3.48_ e. building relationships among new members

_3.05_ f. introducing class members to the church staff

_____ g. other: _____

Figure 8

was considered only "somewhat" a purpose. If relationships were to develop, it would likely be more by accident than by design.

Compare the responses of the class members, though, when asked how membership classes affected their lives (figure 9). On the whole, members indicated that the classes influenced their lives positively. Classes met the primary goal of offering a general orientation to the church, and after the class was completed, members understood better their church's expectations. They likewise learned some doctrine, though they didn't rank gaining doctrinal knowledge as high as learning about the church's expectations.

What caught our research team's attention were the findings related to relationships. Meeting other members and church staff members was not a primary purpose of the membership classes; yet,

INFLUENCE OF A MEMBERSHIP CLASS

Using this scale, indicate how your participation in a new member class influenced your life.

1   2   3   4   5   6   7   8   9   10

Strongly disagree	Disagree	Uncertain	Agree	Strongly agree

_9.07_ a. I now know the church's expectations for its members.

_8.39_ b. I know more about my church now.

_8.29_ c. I am more willing to invite friends to church now.

_8.28_ d. I would be more comfortable talking to my pastor now.

_8.12_ e. I know more people in the church now.

_8.05_ f. I am now more willing to get involved in the church by leading or supporting a ministry of the church.

_7.45_ g. I understand now the church's policy for discipline of its members.

_7.26_ h. I know more about my denomination now.

_7.25_ i. I understand more about baptism and the Lord's Supper now.

_7.11_ j. I am now more willing to give financially to my church.

_6.93_ k. I pray more often now.

_6.87_ l. I know more about God now.

_6.85_ m. I now know my spiritual gift(s).

_6.52_ n. I know more about studying the Bible now.

_6.47_ o. I am more prepared to tell others about Jesus now.

Figure 9

class members plainly viewed relationship building as a benefit of the class. Stephanie, a layperson from Georgia, put it this way: "Meeting people was really important. It [the class] just gives members a chance to know new people on a smaller scale."

Among class members there was often a common bond of excitement and anticipation (as well as, for some new believers, anxiety over beginning the Christian walk). Hence, the most effective classes we studied not only promoted dialogue but also allowed members to get to know each other, pray for each other, and offer encouragement to each other.

Indeed, the classes that produced the strongest relationships did so because they *intended* to do so; that is, they included relationship building in the class structure. Some simple ways to achieve this included having a meal together outside of class, setting up a prayer chain among class members, providing photos and contact information of all members, and utilizing "sponsors" who accompanied new members to the class. The "Getting to Know You" forms (appendixes 2 and 3) may help your church reach this goal as well.

PEOPLE-TO-PASTOR RELATIONSHIPS

Here's how a number of laypeople described the "primary benefits" they received from attending their class:

- It made me very comfortable with the pastor, and in return it was much easier to ask my questions.

  Michael, North Carolina

- Meeting some of the key people and leaders was very helpful.

  Terri, North Carolina

- We met all of the church staff. We don't get many opportunities for that in a large church.

  Bob, Florida

- I also got to see a side of my pastor that really made me feel good.

  Casey, Texas

- We know the pastor and other new members much better.

  George, Arizona

- I gained appreciation and respect for my pastor and his staff.

  Mark, Wisconsin

- I got to know my pastor on a personal basis.

  Gary, Mississippi

- I learned more about our senior and associate pastors.

  Tiffany, Michigan

Do you hear how much class members appreciated spending time with their pastor? Research team leader Matthew Spradlin summarized these findings after interviewing dozens of class members: "Who they most want to get to know is the guy they listen to each week in the pulpit, and this class provides the opportunity. I can't tell you how important this was to people in these classes."

In the relaxed atmosphere of a membership class, church members saw their pastor up close. They had permission to ask questions they couldn't ask during a sermon. They listened as he prayed for them by name. They often learned about his devotional habits and strategies. In the end, the hours spent with the pastor left a significant mark in the lives of these class members.

PASTOR-TO-PEOPLE RELATIONSHIPS

Pastors likewise expressed excitement about relationships initiated in a membership class (like Butch Ikels observed in the opening page of this chapter). To be honest, though, their excitement was not just about meeting people. It was not simply about developing friendships, though that was important. Their excitement was about telling the story of their churches, about talking about what God was doing and challenging others to "get on board."[12] As one leader told us, "I do want to get to know them, but I also want them to get to know us and our vision."

Membership classes provided the venue for these pastors to do both. Pastor Emerson Wiles of Mililani Baptist Church in Hawaii speaks best for all the pastors we interviewed: "I get to spend four hours with every new member. I don't believe there is any way you can put a price tag on that. I learn things about them that would take me years to learn otherwise. Also, they get to spend four hours with me and have the freedom to ask me anything about our church and my beliefs. A trust level is established that might never happen otherwise."

Four hours is not much time, but Pastor Wiles knows the value of spending this time well. Within his church's four-week membership class (called "Basic Steps"), he starts building strong relationships.

A SUGGESTION

We were surprised to find that the senior pastor taught only 71 percent of the classes we studied—and he was not the only teacher in almost half of those classes (table 4). The senior pastor at least made an appearance in most classes, but he did not always assume the responsibility for teaching the class. Yet, listen to the words of Pastor Bill Barnett of Union Hill Baptist Church in Oneonta, Alabama, who does teach at least a portion of his church's class: "I feel it is important for me to establish a strong relationship with our members as soon as possible. This is important, as I will be the one to challenge them to participate in service before the class ends and many times in the future. Even though I have involved other staff and leaders in orientation, *I feel it is too valuable a time to totally delegate to others* [emphasis added]."

On the basis of our research, we strongly encourage senior pastors to teach membership classes. Pastors embody the church's

WHO TEACHES THE NEW MEMBER CLASS?		
Teacher	**Number of churches**	**Percentage**
Senior pastor	20	38.5
Multiple persons, including pastor	17	32.7
Staff member	8	15.3
Layperson	7	13.5

Table 4

vision, and they are most often the driving force behind it. They bring to the class a passion and commitment few others in the church have. And, in most cases, the pastor is one of the best teachers in the church—an important issue, as boring new members to death is not the best way to welcome them to the church!

Pastors who do not lead the classes may miss a prime opportunity to influence church members for years to come. Even a few hours of personal interaction can make a difference.

A QUESTION: CAN RELATIONSHIPS BE BUILT IN FIVE HOURS?

At this point, you may be asking the same question our research team asked: How do you develop relationships in classes that typically meet for an average of a little more than five hours? Further investigation gave us three insights.

First, spending time with the pastor really did affect the new members' lives (have you heard this thought before?). Five hours with the pastor were, in some cases, more time than these members had ever spent with the staff of any church.

Second, strong relationships among class members were more likely to develop in classes that included multiple sessions. Perhaps you remember from the last chapter that 50 percent of the classes we surveyed met for at least four weeks. Longer classes that met over several weeks simply allowed more opportunities for class members to get to know each other.

Finally, relationships that began in the membership classes often remained strong for the laypeople we interviewed. Planned interaction among new members, other small group Bible studies, mutual ministry involvement, and shared life experiences solidified relationships that had begun in membership classes.

In general, members responding to our survey fondly recalled the membership class as the place where they met soon-to-be good friends. This finding helps explain why so many of the laypeople we interviewed were still active in their churches some time after attending membership classes.

RELATIONSHIPS, MEMBERSHIP CLASSES, AND UNINVOLVED MEMBERS

This study affirmed our earlier research project that showed a positive correlation between membership classes and new member retention.[13] That finding, however, still doesn't fully resolve two other problems: the attender who never joins, and the "uninvolved" member who does not serve in the church.

Chapter 6 will address both situations more thoroughly. For now, though, I'll bring this chapter to an end with a membership class model that has proven effective in addressing the latter issue.

A PROPOSED MODEL

As a senior pastor for fourteen years, I sought to get uninvolved members active in the church. Very little worked until our staff developed a "Baptist Beliefs" membership class, which I'd teach four times a year. Several of my pastor friends, including some who participated in this study, have used this model effectively. Our research in this study and in other projects continues to validate its strength.

The class met for thirteen weeks during our Bible study (Sunday school) hour. Thirteen weeks is a long class, but the length was important for reaching our overall goals. Typically, twelve to fifteen persons attended the class. Table 5 outlines the curriculum we followed.

"BAPTIST BELIEFS" CURRICULUM	
Week	**Topics**
Week 1	Introductions; outline of the course
Week 2	History of the church and denomination (including testimonies from long-term members)
Weeks 3–7	Basic beliefs: The Word of God, Theology proper (study of God), Christ and the Holy Spirit, Sin and Salvation, the Church, Baptism and the Lord's Supper
Weeks 8–9	Developing spiritual disciplines
Week 10	Personal evangelism
Week 11	Discovering and developing spiritual gifts
Week 12	Vision of the church; supporting the church through giving
Week 13	Opportunities for service; introductions to staff members, ministry leaders, and Bible study teachers

Table 5

I personally invited attenders from four groups in our church: *guests* who had been attending the church but hadn't yet joined; *new members* who had joined within the last quarter; *uninvolved members* who were attending worship but not attending Bible study or serving in the church; and *long-term involved members* whose faithfulness was a model for others.

Our goals for this class were unique for each group in attendance:

- *Guests* would learn about the church prior to making a decision about membership; thus, potential members would be better informed.
- *New members* would learn early about the church's doctrinal standards and membership expectations. Ideally, of course, new members would know this information prior to joining, but our church hadn't yet made this course a requirement.
- *Uninvolved members* would learn (or perhaps have reinforced) the church's beliefs, while also being personally challenged to get involved.
- *Long-term involved members* would get a refresher course in the church's beliefs, while also serving as a model for others. I often used these people to give testimonies and offer encouragement to the class.

Pertinent to this chapter are the relationships that developed within this class. I had the privilege of getting to know our guests and members better. Indeed, some class members came—including uninvolved members—only because their pastor individually contacted and invited them. In many cases, the uninvolved members were parishioners with whom I had previously spent very little time. A personal letter and a follow-up phone call from the pastor apparently made a difference.

Our uninvolved members also found themselves challenged by others in the class. New members exhibited an excitement that some uninvolved members had lost. Long-term members testified about the joy of service, showing others the benefits of involvement. Over the course of multiple weeks, uninvolved members found it difficult to remain complacent in the context of these new relationships.

In most cases, these uninvolved members also learned the value of a small group. Approximately 60 percent, in fact, joined a small group

Bible study and got involved in ministry after completing the membership class. That's not a bad record for a class I taught for ten years!

My friend Peter comes to mind. Pete had been an uninvolved member of our church for several years. When I invited him to join an upcoming "Baptist Beliefs" class, he surprised me by his enthusiasm. "Pastor, I've had some questions about what we believe. Thanks for taking the time to invite me," he said.

Pete and his wife attended the class and developed a relationship with another older couple who were faithful, long-term members. They later joined the Sunday school class for couples their age. Recognizing that one of his spiritual gifts was hospitality, Pete became the fellowship director for his class. Today he serves in several ministries of the church, making contributions that began when an "uninvolved" member was invited to a membership class.

APPLICATION OF THE MODEL

This model works best in a class that meets for several weeks. There are, though, several principles that can be applied in any membership class that seeks to move uninvolved members into ministry.

- The class must be open to guests and members, and the name of the course must not reflect a limiting to "new members."
- The pastor should take the initiative to enlist class members personally. Hear it again: *Pastoral involvement matters.*
- The class roll should include both uninvolved members and faithful members, in addition to guests and new members.
- The faithful members are critical to the process. Enlist members who are people-oriented and who can enthusiastically communicate their passion for the Lord and the church.
- The class must offer opportunities to discover spiritual gifts and to learn about ways to use these gifts in the church.

- Follow-up is important. This class is only a first step toward increasing the participation of uninvolved members. Introduce class members to leaders of other small groups that are available after the membership class is done.
- Pray about everything! Motivating uninvolved members is a God-sized task.

VELCRO RELATIONSHIPS

Martie, a member at Pastor Wiles's church in Hawaii, was a "missionary kid" who had served on staff at several churches. Listen to her description of the benefits of her church's required membership class: "I think one of the major benefits was getting to spend the time with the pastor and getting to know him and having him get to know me. I also think it helps put all new members on equal footing. These classes were a great way to really get to know the church where we feel God has called us to serve. The time in class also helped us understand some of the points of view of the others in there."

Remember, this class met for one hour a week over four weeks in a course called "Basic Steps." Yet, here was a missionary kid, a lifelong member of her denomination, and a mature Christian who saw the value of the membership class.

Martie told us that the relationships that began in this class were important to her. I suspect her testimony and faithfulness were also an encouragement to the others, even as they studied together the basic tenets of their church's faith.

That kind of Velcro will help church members stick.

HELPFUL APPENDIXES

Appendix 2: "Getting to Know You" Form 1
Appendix 3: "Getting to Know You" Form 2

QUESTIONS FOR CONSIDERATION

1. If your church doesn't have a membership class, what strategy is in place to build relationships in your church? If your church has such a class, are you capitalizing on its potential for building relationships? How? Give some examples.
2. What changes might be needed to strengthen the relationship-building component of your membership class?
3. Who are your church's uninvolved members who need to begin doing ministry? Begin to pray for them.
4. After reading this chapter, what one change or improvement might you make in your church's membership class?

Chapter 4

"What Should We Teach?"

The Curriculum Issue — Doctrine

It was break time at a seminar where I had just finished talking about membership classes. Three pastors immediately cornered me to ask the question I was expecting to hear: "We want to do a membership class, but we can't find good material to use. What do you recommend?"

I had heard this question so many times in conferences I wasn't surprised to hear it in our survey responses as well. Time and again, survey respondents said, "Please be sure to tell us what other churches are doing in their classes. We're always looking for the best resources."

The next two chapters are intended to meet this request. This chapter examines some general findings, followed by a specific look at the *doctrine* taught in these classes. The next chapter centers on the *church expectations* taught, while also reviewing other topics included in these classes.

A Few Preliminaries

Listen to this scenario from one of the churches we studied. Barb became a Christian just weeks before her church was offering their next membership class. She attended the class, excited but frightened because she knew so little about the church and Christianity. In that same class was Alberta, a strong believer who had been a member of her denomination for two decades. She attended the class because it was required, but she wondered if she would learn anything new. Charlie was there as well, the unsaved brother of a church leader. He came to the class, hoping to learn more about "this baptism thing."

If you were leading this class, what would you include in the brief teaching time you had available? Take a moment to look at table 6 to see how the churches we studied answered this question.

Are you surprised by any topics covered in these classes? By subjects *not* covered? Do you wonder about the amount of material included? Perhaps a few more details about these classes will help you understand what we discovered in our research.

NONMEMBERS ALSO ATTEND

In this study, "membership class" or "new member class" by no means meant only members would attend. In fact, just the opposite was true. Ninety-eight percent of the classes allowed nonmembers to attend; 79 percent actually encouraged them to do so (figure 10).

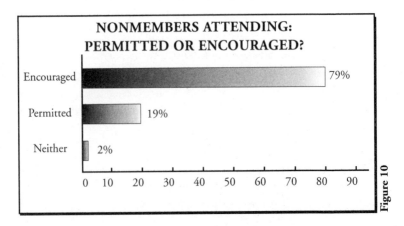

Figure 10

TOPICS ADDRESSED IN A NEW MEMBER CLASS	
Topic	**Percentage of churches**
1. Doctrine of the church	100
2. Expectations of members after joining	96
3. Explanation of the church's mission and/or vision	92
4. Tithing/financial support of the church	88
5. Method and meaning of baptism	86
6. Polity and government of your church	84
7. Requirements for membership	82
8. Plan of salvation	80
9. Purpose of the Lord's Supper	78
10. History of your church	75
11. Current opportunities for service in the church	69
12. Structure/support of missions through the church or denomination	65
13. Introductions to church staff and leadership	61
14. Structure, history, and polity of the denomination	61
15. Examination of the church covenant	57
16. Training in spiritual disciplines (prayer, study, etc.)	51
17. Inventory of spiritual gifts	50
18. Training for witnessing/evangelism	42
19. Tour of the church facilities	28
20. Examination of the church constitution	26
21. Policies for disciplining/excluding members	25

Table 6

"New member class" was the name most commonly used by these churches (46 percent), but the class almost always included non-members.

Three clarifications explain this finding. First, 68 percent of those churches with a required membership class would not formally accept a member until the class was completed (figure 11).

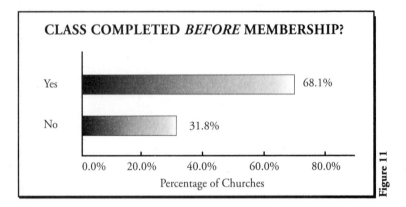

CLASS COMPLETED *BEFORE* MEMBERSHIP?

Yes — 68.1%

No — 31.8%

Percentage of Churches

Figure 11

In some cases, as at Red Mountain Baptist Church in Rougemont, North Carolina, prospective members are received under a six-week watch care period until they have completed the membership class and have been baptized. In churches like Red Mountain, all of the membership class attenders would be classified as "guests." We would rightly assume that orientation, expectations, and some basic doctrinal study would be important in this type of class.

Second, churches that *expected* but did not require a membership class assumed that an informed prospective member would make a better member. The membership class purpose statement for Center Hill Baptist Church of Loganville, Georgia, reflects this philosophy: "The purpose of this class is to encourage you to become an informed member of CHBC so that you may, in turn, become an involved member of CHBC." Churches like Center Hill use the membership class primarily to explain their expectations to potential and new members alike. Ideally, informed nonmembers would become active members, who would go on to get more discipleship and training in other classes.

Third, many churches used the membership class as an intentional evangelistic tool. These congregations strongly encouraged guests to attend the class, where they would hear a personal presentation of the gospel. You'll hear more on this topic later in this chapter.

THE MEMBERSHIP CLASS IS JUST THE BEGINNING

In another Billy Graham School study of effective church leaders, pastors told us that Rick Warren's *The Purpose-Driven Church* heavily influenced their ministries.[14] This impact was also obvious in our study.

Warren's congregation, Saddleback Church in California, uses a four-class "Life Development Process" (designed by Rick Warren) to move persons toward spiritual maturity (figure 12). This process is followed by all who seek membership at Saddleback Church.

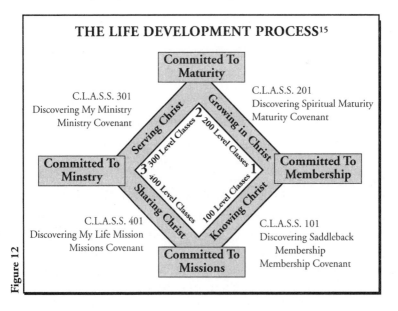

THE LIFE DEVELOPMENT PROCESS[15]

Committed To Maturity

C.L.A.S.S. 301
Discovering My Ministry
Ministry Covenant

C.L.A.S.S. 201
Discovering Spiritual Maturity
Maturity Covenant

Serving Christ — 300 Level Classes — 3

Growing in Christ — 200 Level Classes — 2

Committed To Minstry

Committed To Membership

Sharing Christ — 400 Level Classes — 4

Knowing Christ — 100 Level Classes — 1

C.L.A.S.S. 401
Discovering My Life Mission
Missions Covenant

C.L.A.S.S. 101
Discovering Saddleback Membership
Membership Covenant

Committed To Missions

Figure 12

Class 101 is the membership class, which covers the plan of salvation; baptism and the Lord's Supper; the church's purpose, vision, faith, and values statements; the church's growth strategy; and the organizational structure. Warren's passion for this class is obvious: "I believe the most important class in a church is the membership class because it sets the tone and expectation level for everything else that follows."[16]

Class 201 focuses on developing spiritual disciplines, 301 on determining ministry placement, and 401 on learning to evangelize and do missions. The church's goal is to "turn an audience into an army."[17]

In our study, almost 31 percent of the churches used a 101 class as their membership class. Repeatedly our research team saw the kind of class outline found in Warren's *The Purpose-Driven Church*:[18]

- Our Salvation (the plan of salvation)
- Our Statements (purpose, vision, faith, and values)
- Our Strategy (for growth)
- Our Structure (the church's organization)

Included in most 101 materials were also references to classes 201, 301, and 401—indicating that these churches expected membership classes to be only the starting point toward spiritual maturity.

This trend was obvious even among churches that didn't necessarily follow the Warren model. First Baptist Church of Panama City, Florida, for example, has a three-part discipleship strategy called "DiscipLEARN, DiscipLIFE, and DiscipLEAD." Their goal—"to help persons mature in their faith, equipping them for effective living and serving as a follower of Christ"—could never be accomplished in a single class. Thus, their process begins with a required eight-session membership orientation and continues with courses in their Christian Life Institute.

Many churches we studied had not yet developed such a full-scale discipleship strategy, but no church assumed that the membership class would be the end-all. Consequently, they did not plan for the membership class to cover everything needed for effective Christian living; instead, this class was the place to get the basics.

THE TEACHERS ARE GOOD TEACHERS

Table 6 (page 65) shows that many of these churches covered a significant amount of material in their membership classes. In fact, they faced one of two practical issues as they organized their classes: (1) If they planned a single-session class, how would they cover all the needed material? or (2) If they planned longer, multi-week classes, how would they keep people attending for weeks?

The answer was the same in both cases: A good teacher led the class (in most cases, the pastor). In shorter classes, gifted teachers covered much material; in longer classes, equally talented teachers exhibited a passion that kept people coming back. Hear again a basic lesson from our study: use your best teacher(s) for this class.

WHAT DOCTRINE DID THEY TEACH?

One hundred percent of the churches we surveyed indicated that they covered church doctrine in their membership classes, regardless of the length of the class. Remember, church leaders considered doctrinal teaching a leading purpose of the class, so this finding shouldn't surprise us.

Some classes covered more doctrine than others, of course. For instance, Piner Baptist Church in Morning View, Kentucky, uses the *Basic Bible Truths* resource. This booklet addresses salvation, the believer's security, baptism, the Lord's Supper, the church, the Scriptures, prayer, evangelism, giving, Christ's return, temptation, and Christian responsibility.[19]

> *"The class allows us to give the scriptural foundation for what we believe, teach, and confess, as well as to explain why and how we worship as we do."*
>
> Gary, a Lutheran church leader

At Faith Evangelical Free Church in Woodruff, Wisconsin, the pastor teaches a three-hour class that utilizes his denomination's *Welcome to the Family!* resource. This membership manual includes chapters covering "the Scriptures, God, Jesus, the Holy Spirit, Man and Sin, Salvation, Baptism and the Lord's Supper, the True Church, Local Church Membership, Local Church Government, the Future, and the Resurrection of the Dead."[20]

It would be wrong, though, to assume that most of the churches surveyed taught systematic theology in their membership classes. In some cases, class leaders made only a passing reference to a doctrinal statement included in the class materials. When they did address specific theological subjects, two topics received the most attention: the plan of salvation and the nature of the church.

THE PLAN OF SALVATION

Eighty percent of the surveyed churches taught the plan of salvation in their membership classes. Several churches told us, in fact, that it was unusual to have a membership class *without* someone getting saved. Listen to the stories of some of these churches.

Ingleside Baptist Church in Macon, Georgia, requires a four-hour class for membership. The class is decidedly evangelistic, as evidenced in the class notes: "The goal of this class is to present the gospel of Jesus Christ and unique dimensions of our life together at Ingleside so that under the leadership of the Holy Spirit you will commit yourself to Christ and the Ingleside family." Mike Hickman, associate pastor of membership, told us, "The very first thing we talk about is salvation. In at least half of the monthly classes offered at Ingleside, someone becomes a believer."

Pastor Bob Harrington of Harpeth Community Church in Franklin, Tennessee, told our team about his church's unique approach to membership. The church offers three courses toward membership: "Exploring Christianity" (for seekers not yet ready to become members); "101: Holistic Conversion in the Bible" (designed to address thoroughly the process of conversion); and "201: Congregational Orientation Seminar" (an introduction to the church's beliefs, mission, structure, practices, and ministries). Prospective members are required to attend both 101 and 201, after which they must agree to the church membership covenant. Course 101 is four hours of teaching on conversion, and approximately 20 percent of the attenders are not Christians. For Pastor Harrington, 101 is the church's means to help people understand the "more substantive concepts" of conversion. You will hear more about Harpeth in chapter 8.

You may remember that Chapel Hill Presbyterian Church in Gig Harbor, Washington, calls its membership class "Welcome to the Family." This church asks all participants to complete a pre-class spiritual questionnaire that requires them to evaluate their spiritual condition (see appendix 4). Participants are then challenged to reevaluate their spiritual lives after the class presentation on "What does it mean to be a Christian and live in a growing relationship with Christ?" Executive pastor Stuart Bond told us it is unusual to have a class without one or two new commitments to Christ.

At Hunter Street Baptist Church in Birmingham, Alabama (also featured in chapter 8), Pastor Buddy Gray always presents the gospel in the "Membership Information Class." Pastor Gray has taught the class more than 130 times, and only once has there not been someone converted in the class!

Ingleside, Harpeth, Chapel Hill, and Hunter Street are distinctly different churches, but all illustrate a commitment to share Christ during their membership process. Church leaders told us repeatedly, "Don't miss the evangelistic opportunity a membership class presents. Invite nonmembers, share the gospel, and pray for God to work."

Our research team discovered another benefit of sharing the gospel in a membership class—the modeling of evangelism for class members. We were surprised that only 42 percent of the churches included evangelism training in their classes, especially because so many new believers would have ready access to non-Christian friends. Those classes that did include evangelism training typically taught only a basic approach to sharing one's testimony, dealing with such issues as these:

- What my life was like before Christ
- How I knew I needed Christ
- How I received Christ
- My life since meeting Christ

Upon further investigation, though, we realized that these churches *were* doing at least basic evangelism training through sharing the gospel in class. As leaders walked through the plan of salvation or directed the class through a gospel tract, they modeled evangelism for the others. We would like to have seen more specific evangelism training in these classes, but the transition from sharing the gospel to encouraging others to do the same was a natural one. We'll return to this issue in chapter 7.

In the back of the book, we've included a sample gospel presentation (appendix 5).[21] Your church may choose to use this resource to share the gospel with the participants in your membership class.

THE NATURE OF THE CHURCH

A class that averages five hours in length provides little time for an in-depth look at the doctrine of the church. The churches in our study focused primarily on four concepts about the church: (1) The church is a family; (2) the church is the body of Christ; (3) God expects us to join a church; and (4) church membership includes responsibilities. A sample lesson outline for your use is included in appendix 6.

The Church as a Family

The picture of the church as a family is implied in several places in the New Testament (see 2 Corinthians 6:18; Ephesians 3:14; 1 Timothy 5:1–2). As the family of God, believers are to love, support, and encourage one another. Church membership, then, is more about people than about procedure and protocol.

Not having grown up in a Christian home, how I appreciate those who have welcomed me as a member of the Christian family! Sonney and Christie invited me into their home as if we had known each other all our lives. Lawrence and Katherine loved me like their own son. Mrs. Morgan and Mrs. Reatherford prayed for me as grandmothers for their grandsons. My Christian in-laws, Ralph and Jeanette Harvey, now model a Christian home for me. I understand what Dave, a layperson from Ohio, told our research team: "I feel like I'm a part of something important now."

Remember, relationships are part of the glue that makes church members stick. Doesn't it make sense that these churches emphasized "church as family" in their membership classes?

The Church as the Body of Christ

The second concept of the church emphasized in these classes is the "body of Christ" imagery (1 Corinthians 12:1–31). The apostle Paul put it this way in verse 18 of that chapter: "But now God has placed the members, each one of them, in the body, just as He desired" (NASB).

The church that seeks to be a New Testament church consists of individual members, all under the headship of Christ and each responsible for fulfilling his or her role in the body. Members are not given permission to "warm a pew" and do nothing else, for God places each member in the church for a reason. Paul simply would not have understood the phrase "uninvolved church member."

In the churches we studied, leaders most often connected the "body of Christ" imagery to Christian responsibility. As one pastor told us, "One unfaithful, nonproductive member will weaken the entire body, and we don't want that to happen." To our surprise, though, only 50 percent of the churches included a spiritual gifts inventory in their membership classes. Many simply laid the groundwork in their classes by telling participants they would be expected to serve. *How* these churches moved members into ministry in the body will be addressed in chapter 6.

The Mandate of Church Membership

The third concept these churches stressed in their membership classes builds on the first two: God expects believers to join a local church, through which they develop Christian relationships and use their gifts. A summary of the biblical arguments looks like this:

- Acts 2:41 — Those who followed Jesus were baptized and identified themselves with local believers.
- 1 Corinthians 12:27 — The church is a body, and there cannot be a body without members.
- Ephesians 5:25 — Jesus loved the church and gave himself for it; believers must be equally committed to the church.
- Hebrews 10:25 — The church must regularly gather together.
- Scriptures that address pastoral leadership and oversight imply a recognized congregation (e.g., 1 Timothy 3:5; Hebrews 13:17).
- Scriptures that speak of church discipline suggest some type of formal list or association (e.g., Matthew 18:15–17; 1 Corinthians 5:11–13).

You could argue that these texts imply rather than command local church membership, and you would be correct. The churches in our study, however, did not promote joining only as a response to a biblical command; rather, they emphasized joining as an expression of commitment to God and to a particular group of believers. Membership is a public pledge to find our role in the body, work alongside other members, and hold each other accountable to faithful Christian living.

As we'll see in the next chapter, these churches most often connected the sacred acts of baptism and the Lord's Supper to a membership commitment. The purposes of these ordinances varied by denomination, but the stipulations usually remained the same: these acts were reserved for those who had made a commitment to Jesus Christ and the church.

The truth is, in the churches we studied, membership really does take on significance.

The Responsibilities of Church Membership

Finally, the membership classes we studied stressed that church membership carries responsibility. In fact, all but two of the churches (96 percent) indicated that they address "expectations of members after joining." One church, Peoples Church of Fresno, California, even includes the duties of their members in the church constitution. There, members learn they must preserve the unity of the church, regularly attend its meetings, serve in its ministries, contribute a tithe for its work, guard its name, and pray for and support its leaders.

This issue is so important that the next chapter will focus on the specific expectations this church and the others stressed. Remember, *expectations* is one of the four components to effective assimilation of new members.

A Four-Step Process

First Evangelical Free Church of Ames, Iowa, uses a four-step process toward church membership:

- *Investigation*, where the potential church member learns about the church through a required "Discovery Class"
- *Affirmation*, when the candidate declares his desire to become a church member through completing a membership form

- *Confirmation*, an interview with two elders, including sharing one's personal testimony
- *Celebration*, when the new member is received at a congregational meeting

For most of the churches we studied, the membership class included attenders (and, in some cases, new members) in the "investigation" process. Church leaders therefore deemed it important to stress the fundamentals of salvation and the church. Deeper teachings would come in later classes, but it would all build on the basic theological foundation laid in the membership class.

Membership expectations, however, would not wait for later classes. Our next chapter will take us to that topic.

HELPFUL APPENDIXES

Appendix 4: Spiritual Questionnaire
Appendix 5: Sample Gospel Presentation
Appendix 6: Sample Lesson on the Church

QUESTIONS FOR CONSIDERATION

1. Compare the content of your church's membership class curriculum with the findings in table 6 (page 65). What do you learn from this list?
2. In what context does a nonbeliever hear the gospel in your church? The worship service? Small group? Somewhere else? How could you effectively use a membership class for evangelism?
3. In what context do your leaders teach about the nature of the church? How could your church do this more effectively?
4. After reading this chapter, what one change or improvement might you make in your church's membership class?

Chapter 5

"WHAT SHOULD WE TEACH?"

The Curriculum Issue — Mission and Expectations

David Coleman is the pastor of Crowfield Baptist Church in Goose Creek, South Carolina. When I talked to David about his church's membership class, his enthusiasm was infectious. "It's the most enjoyable thing I've done as a pastor," he said. "For three weeks, I get to brag about the church to prospective or new members."

In the membership class David describes the church's beliefs, ministry philosophy, structure, and vision. At the same time, he raises the bar of membership by explaining what the church anticipates from her members. "I get to know the people, and they get to know the church's expectations," he told me.

Perhaps you recall that "expectations of members" was one of the top three topics addressed in the membership classes we studied (table 7). The last chapter addressed the topic of doctrine, focusing specifically on the plan of salvation and the nature of the church. In this chapter we will look at the other two topics covered in more than 90 percent of the classes studied: (1) membership expectations and (2) the church's mission.

TOP THREE TOPICS ADDRESSED IN A NEW MEMBER CLASS	
Topic	Percentage of churches
1. Doctrine of the church	100
2. Expectations of members after joining	96
3. Explanation of the church's mission and/or vision	92

Table 7

THE MISSION — A STARTING POINT

Several books on church growth emphasize how important it is for a church to have a clear mission or purpose.[22] George Hunter, a longtime church growth leader, says that a "strong mission statement will become the 'driving force' of the organization, shaping decisions, impacting budget priorities, and keeping the church on course over time."[23] The statement itself, notes Hunter, should be brief, simple, general, memorable, and energizing.

Not surprisingly, 92 percent of the churches we studied included an explanation of their mission in their membership classes. Pay attention to some of the "energizing" purpose statements from the churches in our study:

- Sarasota Baptist Church exists to glorify God by sharing the gospel with unbelievers, serving the hurting, equipping believers practically with God's Word, and exalting Jesus Christ in worship while encouraging people to live in an atmosphere of love and grace.

  Sarasota Baptist Church, Sarasota, Florida

- Our mission is to bring people to Christ and help one another become more like him.

  Harpeth Community Church, Franklin, Tennessee

- As disciples, our mission is to cause God great joy by sharing his love with others as we have seen it in Jesus Christ.
  Advent Presbyterian Church, Cordova, Tennessee

- Our purpose is to exalt Christ by faithfully spreading the gospel and equipping believers in Lawrence and Giles Counties and in the world by the power of the Holy Spirit.
  New Prospect Baptist Church,
  Lawrenceville, Tennessee

- The purpose of Manchester Christian Church is to bring glory to God through a great commitment to the Great Commandment and the Great Commission. We believe God is calling us to change New England by turning ordinary people into extraordinary followers of Christ.
  Manchester Christian Church,
  Manchester, New Hampshire

- We will *exalt* God by *evangelizing* (sharing the Good News of Jesus with others), *equipping* (teaching the Bible in preparation for the challenges of today), and *encouraging* (love and care for one another in practical ways).
  North Lanier Baptist Church, Cumming, Georgia

The churches in our study had a clear purpose, and they made that purpose known in their membership class. Hutch Matteson, the senior pastor of North Lanier Baptist Church, helped our research team understand the importance of teaching the church's purpose: "You don't try to fly to Dallas by just jumping on the first airplane you come to in the terminal. You must find out where the plane is going if you are to arrive at your destination. The same is true with the membership class: You must understand where you are going and how you are going to get there."

In essence, the churches we studied used membership classes to declare the direction the church was flying. Prospective members (and, in some cases, new members) then had to decide whether they were prepared and willing to fly in the same direction. While it seldom happened, we did hear about prospective members who chose not to join after learning about the church's intended direction. Pastors who told us these stories lamented the loss of potential members, but they more strongly affirmed how important it is for church members to move in the same direction. Congregations make little progress when the vision is unknown, unclear, or unaccepted.

EXPECTATIONS STATED UP FRONT

I recently talked with a church staff member who is responsible for discipleship in his church. He lamented the fact that, while many churches have a "Saddleback Sam" model (a mythical composite profile) to understand unchurched people,[24] few have a model to illustrate the church's goals in producing mature believers. Most churches expect little from their members, and they usually get what they expect.

The churches in our study are attempting to break this pattern. All but two (96 percent) specifically indicated expectations of members in their membership classes, and they did so because they believe that membership matters.

Patrick Payton, pastor of the rapidly growing Stonegate Fellowship in Midland, Texas, verbalized this philosophy for us: "We just think membership in the church should be taken as seriously as people take membership in country clubs, and we think they ought to know what is expected of them if they join."

The expectations varied by church, but five were most evident in our study. We've summarized them in what we call the Expectation Pentagon (figure 13). Appendix 7 provides a worksheet to help you develop your own pentagon.

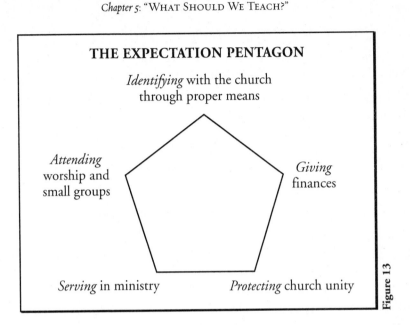

THE EXPECTATION PENTAGON

Identifying with the church
through proper means

Attending worship and small groups

Giving finances

Serving in ministry

Protecting church unity

Figure 13

IDENTIFYING WITH THE CHURCH

In the churches we studied, baptism was the primary means by which members were to identify with the local congregation. The method varied by denomination, but baptism was almost always viewed as a public declaration of one's faith and one's commitment to a local church. In most cases, baptism and church membership were also prerequisites for observing the Lord's Supper.

My friend Kevin Hamm is one of the most creative pastors I know. (Pastor Hamm is one of the pastors who contributed to chapter 8.) His church—Valley View Church in Louisville, Kentucky—gives baptismal invitations for their new members to mail to family members and friends. The invitation reads, "Something special has happened in my life! I want to invite you to celebrate with me! I have accepted Jesus Christ as my Lord and Savior, and I will celebrate this week by being baptized. Please share this special day with me." New members at Valley View quickly become witnesses for Jesus Christ, and they identify with Jesus and with their church through baptism. In one case, forty people came to see a young couple baptized![25]

In several churches we studied, baptism and membership were also preceded by a time of questioning before staff members, elders, or the church body. For example, elders at Advent Presbyterian Church in Cordova, Tennessee, ask seven questions of all who request membership:

1. Do you believe in a personal God who created and sustains all things?
2. Do you believe that human beings in general, and yourself in particular, are spiritually and morally flawed?
3. Do you believe that God has acted to undo the effects of sin (spiritual and moral flaws) by the life, death, and resurrection of Jesus of Nazareth?
4. Do you accept Jesus of Nazareth as your Lord (the one you will follow) and Savior (the one you will rely on to undo the effects of sin in your life)?
5. Do you commit yourself to a life of discipleship as part of a local body of believers (a church) who are trying to live on the basis of God's love shown in Jesus Christ?
6. Do you hope for eternal life in fellowship with God and believe in the ultimate victory of God over sin and death?
7. Do you promise to follow the leadership of this church insofar as we lead it in accordance with Holy Scripture?

New members at Stonegate Fellowship in Midland, Texas, are required to share their testimony with a counselor. Pastor Patrick Payton told us, "There are no gun-barrel confessions at the altar in a few short minutes so everyone can vote on you." Similarly, prospective members at Peoples Church in Fresno, California, share their conversion story with their pastor, who then recommends them for membership.

In these cases and others, the churches were careful to evaluate *who* would be identified with them. Again, they showed us that membership mattered to their congregations.

ATTENDING WORSHIP AND SMALL GROUPS

Our research team wasn't surprised to find that these churches expected their new members to attend worship faithfully. Typical among these churches was this component of the four-point growth strategy for New Prospect Baptist Church in Lawrenceburg, Tennessee: "Exciting celebration services—the church [is] assembled together collectively to be strengthened by the preaching of the Word, to be reinforced in the faith through song, and to express congregational praise to Christ, our audience." The leaders in our study simply believed that worship is a primary purpose of the church, and participation is not optional.

What did surprise us somewhat was that almost 70 percent of the churches used their membership classes to strongly emphasize small group attendance. The membership class notes for East Booneville Baptist Church in Booneville, Mississippi (figure 14), illustrate this emphasis—one we found in many classes.

Like East Booneville, the churches in our study used multiple types of small groups (e.g., Bible study, fellowship, discipleship, support, life needs, accountability, and home cells). Topics and purposes differed, but the groups provided relationships, teaching, and responsibilities—all of which are important components in moving attenders into membership and ministry. One pastor even told us, "If my members have to make a choice between hearing me preach and attending a small group, I want them in the small group."

THE IMPORTANCE OF SMALL GROUPS

I. THE CHURCH REACHING IN THROUGH ORGANIZATION

A. God created the world in an organized manner (Genesis 1).

B. Organizing people for effective ministry is taught throughout the Scriptures.

II. THE CHURCH ORGANIZED THROUGH SMALL GROUPS

A. Moses organized through small groups (Exodus 18:21).

B. Jesus organized through small groups (Luke 10:1).

C. The church organizes through small groups.
- Sunday school
- Discipleship training
- Prayer groups
- Missionary groups

Figure 14

GIVING FINANCES

Some years ago, I asked a church member to share his giving testimony during a stewardship emphasis Sunday. I waited with excitement for him to tell our church how he gave simply because he loved God and could never outgive him. To my great surprise, he began his testimony with these words: "I started tithing as a new Christian because my pastor [me!] told me I had to."

I learned a lesson that day that was to influence the rest of my pastoral ministry: teach and challenge new believers early to be faithful in every area of their lives, including finances. (Sometimes they learn obedience before anyone tells them anything different!)

The churches we studied followed this same philosophy. Eighty-eight percent included in their membership classes a discussion of church financial support, and they weren't afraid to challenge new members to tithe. Though not everyone may agree with these positions, the biblical arguments offered for giving and tithing included the following:

- Leviticus 27:30—a tithe of everything belongs to the Lord.
- Malachi 3:10—the people of God are to bring a tithe into the storehouse.
- 1 Corinthians 16:1–2—the early church received regular offerings.
- 2 Corinthians 9:7—giving was assumed in the early church.

Members of these churches were expected to give systematically (1 Corinthians 16:2) and cheerfully (2 Corinthians 9:7). They were, as stated in one church's covenant, expected to "share the material wealth God has given them." In turn, 65 percent of the laypersons we surveyed said they were more willing to give financially after attending their church's membership class (perhaps that's another good reason to have a class!).

In Fruitland Park, Florida, the leaders of New Life Presbyterian Church promote tithing while also teaching a basic 10-70-10-10 stewardship plan (figure 15). They properly understand that *equipping* must accompany expectations and that new members cannot be expected to live up to standards for which they have no training. This truth is particularly relevant when churches ask new believers to begin setting aside 10 percent of their income for the church. Thus, New Life not only states its expectations but also offers new members a plan for getting there.

THE 10-70-10-10 PLAN

- Ten percent of income (tithe) goes to the Lord's work.
- Seventy percent of income is for the basics.
- Ten percent of income is saved.
- Ten percent of income is set aside for discretionary purposes, including opportunities to give over and above the tithe.

Figure 15

Serving in Ministry

You may remember from the last chapter that the membership classes we studied emphasized the church as a family and as the body of Christ. The final two expectations from the Expectation Pentagon are related to these images.

As the body of Christ, the church is the extension of Christ, who is the Head (Colossians 1:18). We are interconnected and dependent on him and one another. Each member has gifts to be used in the church, and any unfaithful member weakens the entire body. The churches in our study let members know up front that they weren't interested in gaining unfaithful members. Simply put, they expected their members to be workers.

That fact didn't surprise us. What did catch us unawares—as indicated in the last chapter—was that only 50 percent of the surveyed churches included a spiritual gifts inventory in their membership classes. Given that the "body" imagery implies ministry involvement, our team assumed most churches would lead new members to analyze their giftedness, learn about opportunities to serve, and connect their gifts with ministry.

These churches did so, but almost half of them addressed ministry placement in classes other than *membership* classes. The membership classes in these churches provided only orientation, and the gifts inventory would come after prospective members were formally committed to the church. Again, the influence of Rick Warren's 201/301/401 class structure is obvious.

We will address this issue of ministry placement in greater detail in the next chapter. But for those churches that included a gifts inventory in their membership classes, here are some of the resources used:

- *Network Revised*[26]
- Team Ministry Spiritual Gifts Inventory[27]

- Ministry Tools Resource Center Online Spiritual Gifts Test Inventory[28]
- *Finding Your Spiritual Gifts: Wagner-Modified Houts Questionnaire*[29]
- *The BodyLife Journey*[30]

PROTECTING CHURCH UNITY

A short time before he was arrested, Jesus prayed that his followers would be united in their mission (John 17:20–23). Have you ever thought about why he prayed this way? Division in the church is always a threat, and unity comes only by the hand of God. No wonder the churches in our study expected their members to preserve church unity! Members in these churches were to unite around the church's vision and leaders, support small groups, love each other, avoid gossip, and reconcile broken relationships. In essence, they were to protect the family.

Look, for example, at how seriously Cottonwood Church of Albuquerque, New Mexico, approaches this issue:

> Since we are all sinners saved by grace, we hurt each other. Successful church members make a habit of taking the initiative to clear up hurt feelings and damaged relationships. By so doing, they keep their friendships intact and their emotions healthy through the years. . . .
>
> All the leaders at Cottonwood Church commit to reconciling relationships in harmony with Christian principles found in Matthew 5:21–26 and Matthew 18:15–20. At Cottonwood, we've made a commitment to being a *peacemaking church*!

Indeed, Cottonwood expects new members to commit to (1) reconcile conflicts, (2) build five to six relationships with other members, and (3) get involved in ministry as a means to avoid isolation.

Hayward Wesleyan Church in Hayward, Wisconsin, teaches the principles of Matthew 18:15–20 in its membership classes. Doing so informs new members that the church expects them to attempt biblical reconciliation when a relationship is broken. According to class materials, the goal is simple: "Our job is to help (not control) each other. We may have a difference of opinion, but we must maintain unity of heart." Unity is not optional in this church or in others we studied; rather, it is expected.

Often accompanying this call to unity in these churches was a mandate for church members to support their leaders. The leaders in these churches are just that—leaders—and they believe they will answer to God for their ministries. They expect members to pray for them (Ephesians 6:18–20), respect them (1 Thessalonians 5:12–13), and follow them (Hebrews 13:17). When the team follows the leader, unity is that much easier to maintain.

THE USE OF CHURCH COVENANTS

In 57 percent of the churches we studied, most or all of the expectations on the Expectation Pentagon were expressed in a church covenant. As you might assume, several modeled their covenant after that of Rick Warren's Saddleback Church (figure 16).

Our research team also saw covenants that included statements about the church's particular responsibility. For instance, the leaders of Harpeth Community Church in Franklin, Tennessee, make specific commitments to their members (see appendix 8). Leaders at Valley Baptist Church in Bakersfield, California, must covenant to *agree* with the church's faith and practices; *abstain* from intoxicating beverages, tobacco, drugs, abortion, and pornography; *attend* services, meetings, and training opportunities; and *advance* the church by maintaining personal and family devotions, religiously training their children, and sharing their faith. Co-pastor Roger Spradlin tells more about this exciting church in chapter 8.

THE SADDLEBACK MEMBERSHIP COVENANT[31]

Having received Christ as my Lord and Savior and been baptized, and being in agreement with Saddleback's statements, strategy, and structure, I now feel led by the Holy Spirit to unite with the Saddleback church family. In doing so, I commit myself to God and to the other members to do the following:

1. I WILL PROTECT THE UNITY OF MY CHURCH
   - by acting in love toward other members
   - by refusing to gossip
   - by following the leaders

2. I WILL SHARE THE RESPONSIBILITY OF MY CHURCH
   - by praying for its growth
   - by inviting the unchurched to attend
   - by warmly welcoming those who visit

3. I WILL SERVE THE MINISTRY OF MY CHURCH
   - by discovering my gifts and talents
   - by being equipped to serve by my pastors
   - by developing a servant's heart

4. I WILL SUPPORT THE TESTIMONY OF MY CHURCH
   - by attending faithfully
   - by living a godly life
   - by giving regularly

Figure 16

The covenant of East Booneville Baptist Church in Mississippi also reflects a relationship between the church and new members (figure 17).

Church leaders in our study told us that a covenant is important because it puts expectations in writing. What they told us next, though, revealed the difficulty of church covenants: they are easy to write but tough to enforce.

COVENANT:
EAST BOONEVILLE BAPTIST CHURCH

THE CHURCH FAMILY COVENANTS TO LOVE YOU BY:
- teaching you the Word of God
- providing opportunities for growth, nurture, and service
- providing a framework for building fellowship and godly relationships
- carrying out our responsibility to reprove, exhort, care for, and discipline
- broadening the believer's concern and perspective toward those unreached by the gospel

I COVENANT TO LOVE THE CHURCH FAMILY BY:
- growing spiritually
- being faithful in attendance and participation
- supporting the ministries of the church through giving and service
- seeking to preserve the unity of the church

Figure 17

Our research did not provide an easy answer to this issue. You may remember from chapter 1 that, in their membership classes, only 25 percent of the churches addressed policies for disciplining and excluding members. Most of the churches we studied admitted that their expectations were just that—*expectations* rather than *requirements*. They stressed expectations, but they hadn't yet fully resolved how to hold their members accountable to the covenant.

If we saw any trend with regard to holding members accountable, it was accountability through small groups or specific ministry leaders. One church attempting to enforce accountability is Oak Hill Baptist Church in Griffin, Georgia. Oak Hill expects all Sunday school teachers and ministry leaders to hold members accountable, and "life stage pastors" work to assure that all are serving faithfully. Ministry team leaders are responsible for contacting members at least once a month and reporting in detail to the appropriate life stage pastor. These pastors submit written monthly reports to the senior pastor. With this type of accountability, the church has grown from eighty members in 1993 to 2,700 in 2004!

RAISE THE STANDARDS

Despite the struggle these churches faced with accountability, their membership classes still raised the standards of church membership. Eugene, a layperson from South Carolina, expressed thoughts similar to those we heard from others: "Through our membership class, I learned about our church covenant and about the expectations God and my church have of me." That fact alone probably puts Eugene ahead of most church members in America today.

An effective membership class lays the foundation for church members to participate fully in the life of the church. Raise the standards of church membership; promote these standards through an intentional class—and then expect people to live up to them. The church may well be stronger than it has ever been.

At the same time, what do you do with the persons who will not join? Or with the members who will not serve? We turn to those topics in the next chapter.

HELPFUL APPENDIXES

Appendix 7: The Expectation Pentagon Worksheet
Appendix 8: Sample Membership Covenant

QUESTIONS FOR CONSIDERATION

1. What is your church's mission statement? If you don't have one, work with leaders to develop one that is brief, simple, general, memorable, and energizing.
2. What does your church expect from new members? Are these expectations written down somewhere?

3. If your church has a covenant, how could it be strengthened? If your church doesn't have one, what kinds of things would you suggest be included in a covenant?
4. After reading this chapter, what one change or improvement might you make in your church's membership class?

Chapter 6

"But What about Those Who Still Don't Get Involved?"

The Enlistment Issue

———

Tony Dungy, coach of the Indianapolis Colts football team, once said, "I like expectations. But if all you do is talk, you can lose sight of where you're going."[32] Talking *without doing* leads to unfulfilled expectations.

The churches in our study were not interested in only talking about expectations. While recognizing their need to improve accountability, they expected members to live up to the standards we examined in the last chapter. Prospective and new members learned early on about those expectations.

That's not to say, however, that these churches never faced obstacles. They sometimes dealt with members who would not serve. Other church leaders who heard about our study also voiced frustration about attenders who simply never joined. This chapter addresses both of these topics.

WHY DON'T THEY JOIN?

In 2001, one of the largest studies of congregations ever done in the United States showed that 10 percent of the people sitting in pews on Sunday morning were not members of any congregation.[33] Another study revealed that 10 percent of Americans attend church more than six times a year but are not members of any church.[34]

Several factors may explain this reality. In some cases, attenders are skeptical about the church in general. They are seeking authenticity, and thus "courting" the church to determine if it is *real* is a logical step for them. Others who have suffered wounds in former congregations aren't willing to make an investment in a new church. They attend, but attending does not necessarily involve an emotional commitment to that congregation. Still others want religion—but not *institutional* religion. They are among those who are spiritual but not religious, those who want spirituality without accountability to the church.

Our transient society likely contributes to this problem as well. Census Bureau data tells us that over 40 million Americans move each year, and most move once every five years or so.[35] Why commit myself to a church if I know I might be gone in a couple of years?

In other cases, it is likely that church attenders do not know how to become church members. I visit dozens of churches every year, and seldom do I hear anyone explain how to join the church. I hear about salvation (and obviously that's the most important), about church programs, and about church prayer concerns—but I cannot recall the last time a church leader explained clearly the process of membership. If I were an unchurched person looking to join, how would I know where to get that information?

So how do we respond to those pastors and leaders who asked us what we were learning about moving attenders into membership? Simply this: we admit this problem is a real one, and it can be a frustrating one indeed. But it is also a problem that *can* be addressed and corrected to a large extent. Let's turn to what the churches in our study taught us.

Moving Attenders into Membership

This study began as a look at church membership classes in growing churches. When others asked about getting attenders to join in the first place, we sought further insights from our surveyed churches and from other congregations as well.

You may remember from chapter 1 that few of these churches faced a significant problem with attenders who never joined. Instead, many joined these churches *because leaders let it be known that membership matters in their congregations*. Those who chose not to stay in the church did so for the same reason: membership mattered, and they weren't interested in making that kind of commitment.

Does this mean, then, that these churches had nothing to teach others about moving attenders into membership? On the contrary, our team heard five underlying assumptions we believe will help other congregations motivate long-term attenders to join.

People Are Taking Longer to Join a Church

One study has shown that on average, attenders come to church for eighteen months before they join.[36] None of our survey respondents spoke in terms of that length of time, but several said attenders seldom decide quickly to join a church.

Interestingly, several leaders told us that their churches do very little to "convince" people to join or to hurry them along in their decision process. On one hand, the churches are growing enough that they don't need to hurry those who are deliberating membership; on the other hand, membership *does* matter to these churches, but they do not want coerced members. Ultimately, they want members who, as one North Carolina minister of education told us, "want to belong to something worthwhile—even if it takes some time for them to get there."

Douglas New, pastor of Mt. Pleasant Baptist Church in Carrollton, Georgia, echoed those words. His experience shows that attenders may take longer to join, but "they really want to be a part of a church that is making a difference in the community and world." Sometimes attenders just take a while to determine if the church is really making a difference.

These churches taught us that *patience* is a key to moving attenders into membership. Gone are the days when people quickly joined their denomination's church closest to their home. Those leaders I call "microwave church growth leaders"—who aren't happy unless all of their goals for tomorrow were met yesterday—will likely be uncomfortable with this reality.

PEOPLE WILL JOIN EXCITING CHURCHES THAT STRIVE FOR EXCELLENCE

In the city where I reside—Louisville, Kentucky—is the Southeast Christian Church, one of the largest churches in America. Every time I attend Southeast, I am amazed by the enthusiasm and the quality with which their members do their tasks.

Pastor Bob Russell reports that 90 percent of their members invited someone to come to church with them in a given year. They did so "because they are excited about what they've experienced and are confident that every week the grounds, the nursery, the greeting, the singing, and the preaching will be done with excellence."[37] At Southeast, excited members invite guests, who often then become members themselves.

The churches in our study showed this same pattern. In fact, even the membership class materials sent to us were, for the most part, top-notch. Bob Russell's words are again challenging: "Often your first effort at a new task becomes the standard for later expectations. If you make all A's in your first semester of college, you've established a standard.... Determine that the first time you try something new at your church, it's going to be the best it can be done."[38]

The churches we studied understood that their membership classes provided, in many cases, their first focused opportunity to show prospective members they believed in excellence. No wonder one pastor told us, "Make this event a premier, high-quality event! The best teacher, the best child care, the best prepared materials, the best schedule, even the best snacks—all these set a high standard of quality for prospective and new members."

These churches were passionate about doing ministry with excellence, and attenders eventually wanted to be a part of that work. If I were a guest at your church this week, would I sense that your congregation is committed to excellence?

PEOPLE WILL JOIN IF THEY KNOW THE BENEFITS OF BEING IN THE FAMILY OF GOD

A Nazarene church membership manual from the 1970s said this about the church: "In the family [the church] you find support, love, and strength.... From your brothers and sisters in Christ you receive encouragement and the sense of belonging. The collective strength of God's family is yours."[39] How much more relevant are these words today, when relationships are so often broken? Membership in churches that emphasize *family* really does matter (figure 18).

Chapter 4 examined the biblical support for membership that these churches taught in their membership classes. In addition to the Bible's teachings, these classes emphasized the relational benefits of church membership (once again, it's the relationship thing!). Charles Ransdell, pastor at Edgewood Baptist Center and Chapel in Dayton, Ohio, understands the importance of "family building" in his congregation. Edgewood is an inner-city congregation that meets in a high-crime area, yet their congregation of 125 reached more than fifty converts during the year of our study. Pastor Ransdell told our team, "Our church doesn't emphasize membership by itself.

WHY JOIN A CHURCH?

CHURCH MEMBERSHIP
- is a person's public commitment to a particular group of believers
- allows church leaders to fulfill their task of shepherding those who have joined the church
- defines and builds the team that is ready to do the work of the church
- offers a support system when believers are tempted or struggling
- provides opportunities for spiritual growth under the guidance and accountability of other church members
- challenges believers to use their God-given spiritual gifts alongside others God has placed in the church
- grants permission to believers to offer input and direction for a local church body
- provides a family in a rapidly changing society

Figure 18

'Membership' is for clubs." Instead, membership in this congregation is about belonging and about finding a family. That was a story we heard throughout our study.

MEMBERSHIP EXPECTATIONS DO NOT HINDER GROWTH

Listen to these words from Bill Gambrell, a staff member at Johnson Ferry Baptist Church in Marietta, Georgia: "We let them [attenders] know they are welcome and that we want them at the church, but we tell them up front that we are a 'high expectation' church. We share with them our membership expectations. We also tell them ... that our church may not be the church for them."

Do you think this strong approach to church membership hinders growth? Consider this: During the year of our study, Johnson Ferry added 490 members to their rolls; more than 250 were new converts who joined through baptism.

The numbers differ, but many churches in our study can tell similar stories. One staff member from Tennessee summarizes the gist of what they said to us: "We emphasize the biblical responsibilities and purpose of membership, and people *still* join." As you've heard throughout the book, raising the bar of church membership did not keep these churches from growing.

THE MEMBERSHIP CLASS IS THE PLACE TO EMPHASIZE MEMBERSHIP

This is one of the most significant findings for our research team: these churches emphasized their *membership classes* more than they did membership. In some cases, of course, the class was required for membership; in many other cases, however, the class served as an outreach tool.

The point is, these churches believed they could move attenders into membership *if they could get them to attend membership classes*. Leaders believed so passionately in what they were doing that they just assumed others would capture their vision and join the team. For that reason, these churches broadly emphasized membership classes. Pastors wrote personal invitations to attend, staff members announced membership class opportunities from the pulpit, and administrative assistants included announcements in church newsletters and bulletins. In some churches, "encouragers" assigned to prospects enlisted them and attended the class with them. These strategies worked quite well, as more than two-thirds of the members who joined these churches in the two years before our study had attended membership classes.

Before we look at how churches motivate members to do ministry, let's sum up this chapter thus far. The churches we studied aimed for excellence, raised the membership bar, and emphasized the relational benefits of joining. They highlighted membership through classes they prioritized and promoted. If your congregation has large numbers of attenders who have not joined, what message is your church sending them? Do they know that *membership matters* to your congregation?

MOVING MEMBERS INTO MINISTRY

Getting attenders to join the church is only a first step in moving them into ministry. In fact, moving them to ministry is sometimes even more difficult.

When our team asked leaders how their churches moved members into ministry, we often heard responses like this one from Bob Carpenter, pastor of Cedar Street Church in Holt, Michigan: "This is not an area of strength for us, but we're working to develop a better program." Seldom did we hear from a leader who was completely satisfied with the church's process for ministry placement.

Yet, our analysis of the data indicates that the churches in our survey were doing better than they thought in involving members in ministry. On average, 69 percent of the new members who joined these churches in the last two years attended membership classes. Notice, then, our findings after asking the follow-up question, "What percentage of members who have joined within the last two years are currently active in the church—attending worship at least twice a month and involved in some other type of activity or ministry in the church?" (figure 19).

In the churches we surveyed, over 70 percent of the members who joined in the last two years remained involved in the church. Our research did not ask specific details about the "type of activity or ministry"; nor can we show that the 70 percent who remained involved were only those who attended membership classes. Nevertheless, we are confident these churches point to some important principles for moving members into ministry.

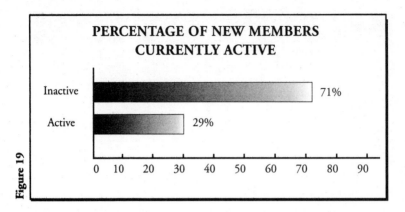

Figure 19

A MINISTRY PLACEMENT STRATEGY MUST BE IN PLACE

Fifty percent of the churches we studied used a spiritual gifts inventory in their membership classes (see page 65), and most of the remaining churches did so in follow-up classes. Never, though, did we see a church that relied exclusively on the inventory as the means of ministry placement.

Indeed, our team often saw placement processes based on Rick Warren's SHAPE concept, Wayne Cordeiro's DESIGN program, or the *BodyLife* model (table 8). Pastors like Saddleback's Warren, and Cordeiro, who leads New Hope Christian Fellowship in Honolulu, Hawaii, challenge their members to discover their spiritual gifts only in the context of looking holistically at themselves. God works through our life experiences, our desires, our spiritual gifts, our personalities, and our abilities in order to prepare us to do ministry in his church.

Whether in a membership class or another class, new members in our study were led to ask, "How has God created me, molded me, and changed me so that I am who I am—ready to be further equipped for service?" Gifts inventories, personality tests, and personal interviews were typically part of the process. The DISC profile was one of the more popular personality tests utilized by these churches.[40]

MINISTRY PLACEMENT PROCESSES[41]		
The SHAPE Process	**The DESIGN Process**	**The *BodyLife Journey* Process (SERVE)**
Spiritual gifts—how has God gifted me?	**D**esire—what is my passion?	**S**piritual gifts—how has God gifted me?
Heart—what are my passions?	**E**xperiences—what experiences in life have helped to make me who I am?	**E**xperiences—what experiences in life have helped to make me who I am?
Abilities—what can I do?	**S**piritual gifts—how has God gifted me?	**R**elational style—what behavioral traits does God use to help me relate to others?
Personality—what is my personality type?	**I**ndividual style—what is my personality temperament?	**V**ocational skills—what abilities have I gained through experience and training?
Experiences—what experiences in life have helped to make me who I am?	**G**rowth phase—where am I in my personal spiritual journey?	**E**nthusiasm—what passion do I have for certain ministry areas?
	Natural abilities—what can I do?	

Table 8

First Southern Baptist Church of Salina, Kansas, is one of the surveyed churches that uses the *BodyLife Journey* program for ministry placement. *BodyLife* is an intentional discipling process designed to guide believers into ministry. Associate pastor Mike Murray told us that each new member is assigned an encourager, who plays a key role in getting the member to attend a *BodyLife* workshop.

There, each new member develops his or her SERVE profile and maps out a "Personal Action Plan" for getting involved in the church. The action plan includes commitments to support corporate and personal worship, evangelize the lost, attend discipleship courses, build relationships through a small group, and minister based on one's SERVE profile. Like so many of the churches we studied, their ministry placement strategy is an *ongoing process* that requires commitment and accountability.

THE BEST RECRUITING FOR MINISTRY IS FACE-TO-FACE

In our study, 76 percent of the laypeople we surveyed indicated they were "more willing to get involved in the church" after attending membership classes. Let's let some of the laypeople tell us why they began to do ministry through their church:

- A minister spoke to me and challenged me to get active.
  Danny B.

- The minister of education sat me down and talked to me.
  Kevin E.

- Two guys approached me and asked me [to serve].
  Don L.

- Brother Sal helped plug me in to ministry.
  Kelly C.

- The leaders invited me, and I prayed about it.
  Rhonda N.

- I received encouragement from a Sunday school teacher and a deacon.

Cindy L.

Do you hear what led these members to serve? A personal challenge and invitation made the difference. Seldom did we hear from churches that recruited volunteers only by pulpit announcements, newsletter requests, or sign-up sheets on the bulletin board.

Lutheran Church of the Redeemer in Birmingham, Michigan, is one example of a church that recruits personally. New members first complete a "Ministry Opportunities Checklist" provided in their membership orientation. Staff member Gary Priskorn distributes the checklists to the appropriate ministry leaders, who then contact the interested members. And, if new members desire, this church links them with "new member sponsors" who shepherd them into ministry involvement. Gary's goal is that new members are actively serving in one ministry within the first six months of membership. For that reason, he then follows with another personal contact, helping to assure that members get involved.

If you think about it, many of the churches we surveyed recruited ministry participants like Jesus did: face-to-face and one-to-one (e.g., Matthew 4:18–22; Mark 2:14). It makes sense that this method would be effective.

ENTRY-LEVEL MINISTRY POSITIONS ARE IMPORTANT

At Stonegate Fellowship in Midland, Texas, participants in the required "Newcomers Class" receive a notebook that includes a detailed list of service opportunities. Similar to many other churches we studied, Stonegate asks those interested in membership to complete a form indicating where they might be willing to serve.

Specifically, adult assimilation pastor Mike Goeke emphasized the "shallow end" ministry opportunities the church offers. "When we say 'shallow end,'" observed Mike, "we mean areas of service that do not require spiritual maturity or knowledge and where, as a result, there is minimal risk of wrong teaching or personal, spiritual damage. Our hospitality (greeting, coffee/refreshments, children's area registration, welcome center, escorts) and parking ministries are entirely 'shallow end.'"

"Shallow end" ministries at Stonegate serve several functions. First, members can get plugged in quickly. Second, those who are unsure of where they should serve have opportunities to experiment. Third, church leaders can test the "servant quotient" of other potential leaders by seeing if they are willing to serve first in the "shallow end." Rarely does anyone serve in a teaching position at Stonegate who hasn't served in the "shallow end."

Hayward Wesleyan Church in Wisconsin follows a similar process. Entry-level opportunities include folding newsletters, cutting the lawn, helping the needy, and serving as greeters. These "support roles" give everyone an opportunity to serve.

Researcher Win Arn has found that growing churches have a minimum of sixty tasks or roles available for every hundred adults, with little overlap in the roles.[42] Entry-level, "shallow end" responsibilities—where even the newest member can feel needed—offer one way to work toward the goal of moving people into ministry.

RECOGNITION AND AFFIRMATION MATTERS

I love what Jack Allen, pastor of Cottonwood Church in Albuquerque, New Mexico, told us: "We make heroes out of our members. We invite them up front. We talk about their personal and spiritual growth. We celebrate their commitments to serve. We make heroes out of the people we want others to emulate."

I suspect (1) it is fun to serve at Cottonwood, where service is publicly recognized, and (2) more members serve there simply because they know they are appreciated. The churches in our study taught us that creating an atmosphere of affirmation increases the willingness to serve. Robert Dale, author of *Pastoral Leadership*, describes this truth well: Members who serve well are those who are "well paid in 'thank-yous' and positive reinforcements."[43]

Does your church affirm those who serve? Consider the following list, first promoted by a Sunday school worker in the Assemblies of God USA:[44]

- Give simple gifts, like a note, a card, a homemade muffin, or a candy bar.
- Give workers name tags on a recognition day so the church will see how many are currently serving.
- Create a bulletin board or a multimedia presentation that shows workers in action.
- Surprise workers with a continental breakfast or pizza lunch.
- Print testimonies of lives changed through the ministry of church workers.

A REVIEW

A brief review of the lessons of this chapter can help us see why so many churches struggle with moving members into ministry. Read through table 9, and determine where your church stands on this issue.

EXPECTATIONS AND RESULTS

Sam is a seventy-six-year-old church member who has served as a teacher, deacon, and visitation leader in his church. He told us, "People want to serve, but they need to be asked and need to know how." Our research shows Sam is correct.

Though they saw room for improving their processes, the churches we studied expected attenders to join and then encouraged members to serve. One-to-one, they led members to discover their passions and gifts, gave them immediate opportunities to serve, and affirmed their commitment. In the end, faithful members most often found their place, knowing they were a part of something that really mattered.

CHURCHES THAT PEOPLE JOIN	
Churches that struggle with those who remain attenders and with members who are uncommitted—	**Churches where people join and serve—**
may have expectations but do not state them clearly or consistently	clarify expectations up front
often accept mediocrity	demand excellence
fail to build on the church's relational nature	emphasize and strengthen relationships
may have a membership class but fail to capitalize on its value	use a membership class to promote joining and serving
tend to emphasize only spiritual gifts (if anything) in ministry placement	have a strategic plan for leading members to see their overall spiritual makeup
recruit workers by broad announcements with little personal attention	recruit workers one-to-one
have a tendency not to think creatively about ministry opportunities, focusing only on positions already in place	provide entry-level positions for workers, even if they are new positions "outside the box"
take their workers for granted	affirm and celebrate their workers

HELPFUL APPENDIXES

Appendix 9: Ministry Opportunities Checklist
Appendix 10: "Discovering Your Ministry" Worksheet

QUESTIONS FOR CONSIDERATION

1. In your opinion, why do attenders in your church not join? Why do members not serve?
2. If your church has a membership class, what is the process for enlisting participants? How can it be strengthened?
3. How can your church improve its strategy for moving members into ministry?
4. After reading this chapter, what one change or improvement might you make in your church's membership class?

Chapter 7

"WHERE DO WE START?"
The Transition Issue

Maybe you're a fan of jigsaw puzzles. I'm not, because I'm not a very patient person. The thought of spending hours (or days or weeks) putting together little puzzle pieces in order to create a picture you can do little with makes no sense to me. If I want a new picture, I'd much rather run to the discount store, purchase one, and have it on the wall within a couple of hours!

But I must admit that leading a church through change can at times feel like putting together a jigsaw puzzle. For example, you need to know where you are headed—that is, what do you want the picture to look like when the change is completed? You must be willing to work slowly and methodically, putting the picture together piece by piece. When the pieces don't quite fit, you must patiently figure out how each piece fits into the overall picture. And you cannot give up until the picture is complete.

The goal of this chapter is to help you put the puzzle together as you lead your church to move attenders into membership and ministry. If the puzzle pieces sometimes seem overwhelming, remember that in the final picture your church will be much stronger.

STARTING A MEMBERSHIP CLASS

Steve Sjogren, the launching pastor of the Vineyard Community Church in Cincinnati, Ohio, writes that *simple* and *effective* are "two words that ought to go together in the church."[45] These simple, effective steps should help you begin a membership class in your church.

PRAY FOR GOD'S WISDOM AND DIRECTION

Leading a church is a God-given task that demands his strength and guidance. Bathe this entire membership process in prayer. God, too, wants church members to live up to his expectations.

DECIDE TO PAY THE PRICE FOR MAKING MEMBERSHIP MATTER

Change is seldom easy. And unless you are planting a church, raising the membership bar will likely necessitate some change in your congregation. An effective membership class will require additional time in your schedule. Equipping current members for service may be time-consuming and energy-draining. Holding members accountable can be frustrating—even painful—when tough decisions must be made about unfaithful members.

Furthermore, churches that systematically raise the standards of membership sometimes see a temporary plateau or decline in new members. Prospective members who might have joined had there been no requirements simply choose to join other congregations. The decrease is usually temporary, but church leaders accustomed to consistent growth often don't rest well during the transition period.

The church leaders we surveyed stressed that raising the membership bar is well worth the cost. Notice, for instance, how they evaluated the work involved in a membership class (figure 20).

All but one of the fifty-two churches involved in our study disagreed or strongly disagreed with the statement "A new member class is too much work to make it worthwhile." The same number

---

VALUE OF A MEMBERSHIP CLASS
Using the following scale, respond to each
of the statements below:

1	2	3	4	5
Strongly disagree	Disagree	Uncertain	Agree	Strongly agree

1.21 A new member class is too much work to make it worthwhile.

4.65 Our church is a stronger church because we have a new member class.

Figure 20

---

and percentage (98 percent) indicated that a membership class strengthened their church.

Other leaders spoke energetically and passionately about the value of moving new members into ministry through membership classes. The Church at Crossgate Center in Hot Springs, Arkansas, began requiring a membership class after an ad hoc vision team recommended the change. Pastor Chuck McAlister teaches the class, which includes spiritual gifts discovery and ministry placement. The pastor told our team that the class has generated an excitement and anticipation not previously experienced by new members. The back door is closing as new members get plugged in to ministry.

Another pastor told us about the joy of watching longer-term members get involved in ministry. "As we've intentionally gone after our uninvolved members," he noted, "it's been fun to see the sitters become the workers. These members are more excited than I've ever seen them."

Moving attenders into membership and members into ministry through a membership class will require some work. Decide now that the results are worth the cost.

GET YOUR LEADERS ON BOARD

Very few churches in our survey indicated that they faced significant opposition or obstacles to implementing membership classes. Listen, though, to a few sources of opposition, albeit weak:

- "Some church members had reservations about requiring it for membership."
- "Some older members wondered if they would be required to take the course."
- "Some people thought we would run others away so they wouldn't join."
- "A few members considered a membership class to be legalistic."

Regrettably, in many cases, the strongest opposition to establishing membership classes came from vocal leaders within the church.

Of course, seldom does change last if key leaders aren't in favor of the change. Here are some simple, effective strategies to get your leaders on board:

Do a study of the assimilation of new members in your church. In the churches we studied, 71 percent of the members who joined in the past two years remained active in the church. How many members who joined your church in the last year are actively serving in the church today? The past two years? Five years? If your leaders see a poor assimilation track record, they may be willing to address the situation.

Select a few leaders to read this book. At the risk of sounding self-serving, I hope this book will lead churches to make sure that membership matters to their congregations. Perhaps reading this book will help leaders learn from other churches that have raised the membership bar.

Preach and teach about the importance of active church involvement. If you do this, you will not only show the importance of teaching new members, but you'll also be challenging uninvolved members to get busy in the church. In chapter 1, I told the story of Will Langford, a pastor who successfully strategized ways to move uninvolved members into ministry. Trusting the Word of God to challenge the uninvolved members, Pastor Langford preached a three-week series of messages titled "A Priestly Purpose" (1 Peter 2:4–10), "Fully Loaded [for Ministry]" (Ephesians 4:9–16), and "The Body of Christ" (1 Corinthians 12:12–31).[46] The Word of God is "living and active. Sharper than any double-edged sword, it penetrates even to dividing soul and spirit, joints and marrow; it judges the thoughts and attitudes of the heart" (Hebrews 4:12). Why not use that Word to encourage active church participation? To help you do so, see the sample sermon outline from 1 Corinthians 12 in appendix 11.

Work with leaders to determine the best type of class for your church. Will the class seek to accomplish a more *informational* or *instructional* purpose? What might be the best time to offer the class? Who should attend the class? Who will teach it? What content should be covered? Involve some leaders in the development of the course, and they will likely be much more supportive.

Test-run the membership class with several leaders. As a young pastor who wanted to lead my church to adopt a membership class, I asked the deacons to be my "test class." They graciously endured my teaching and gave me helpful feedback—and then they strongly encouraged the church to make this course a part of the membership process. We did not require the class, but our deacons so enthusiastically promoted it that few new members failed to attend.

DEVELOP A PLAN TO TEACH THE COURSE TO ACTIVE MEMBERS

Peninsula Baptist Church in Mooresville, North Carolina, averaged 452 in Sunday school and 560 in worship during the year of our study. Peninsula's 101 class regularly meets once every two months. To make certain that all adults had completed a membership class, though, each Sunday school class also taught the 101 curriculum. The church's minister of education David Simon told our team that this approach not only trained many more members but also "heightened the importance of the membership process."

Other churches we studied used a Sunday evening or midweek service to teach the membership curriculum to current members. The membership class would meet at a different time, but they first taught the material to the greatest number of active members.

Our team found four significant benefits to this plan:

1. This approach does (as David Simon told us) emphasize the importance of membership training. A church that sets aside time during Sunday school or service time to teach a membership curriculum says clearly that *membership matters*.

2. This process answers the question "If we implement a membership class, will we expect current members to take it too?" Long-term members are less inclined to participate in membership classes voluntarily, and few churches are willing to *require* them to attend. But teaching the material during a regular gathering time allows long-termers to get the training without requiring them to attend a class.

3. Uninvolved members are again challenged to find their place in ministry through the church. In too many cases, long-term members aren't doing much in ministry. They've grown accustomed to attending without serving. This approach provides another opportunity to remind them of their responsibility to get involved in the church.

4. Members who know the value of the class curriculum are more inclined to encourage others to attend the class. A satisfied "graduate" of the class becomes the best recruiter for future classes.

START THE CLASS, AND STICK WITH IT

The original survey in our study asked growing churches if they had membership classes. Fifty-two churches did; nineteen churches said they didn't yet have such a class. In some cases, these churches previously had membership classes but dropped them. Finding a workable time slot was difficult. Attendance was sporadic. Good curriculum was hard to find. Instead of working out the details, a few churches just gave up on developing membership classes.

On average, the classes we studied had been in existence for 5.6 years. Leaders were committed to making classes effective, and they fought off any temptation to discontinue them. Mark O. Wilson, pastor of Hayward Wesleyan Church in Wisconsin, best expressed this commitment when we asked his advice for other pastors considering membership classes: "Go for it! Be consistent! This is a great time to challenge people to a higher commitment. Don't settle for the lowest commitment level. Challenge them in tithing, service, spiritual depth, community—all of these are important."

BEGINNING THE PROCESS OF MOVING MEMBERS INTO MINISTRY

Chapter 6 provided a number of guidelines for moving members into ministry:

- Help members determine their SHAPE or DESIGN.
- Recruit them one-on-one.
- Provide entry-level opportunities.
- Affirm those who serve.

The question now is, "How do we start this process?" The following principles should get you moving in the right direction.

BUILD EXPECTATIONS AND MINISTRY PLACEMENT INTO YOUR MEMBERSHIP PROCESS

You probably expected this principle by this point in the book. My point is simply to emphasize again what I said in chapter 1: The time to move members into ministry is *when they first join the church.*

Thus, you should employ a two-pronged approach to moving members into ministry. Primarily, you'll want to get new members busy quickly so they have little opportunity to become uninvolved members. At the same time, you must begin to implement a strategy for motivating your uninvolved members. The remaining principles in this section address this issue.

ENLIST A PRAYER TEAM TO PRAY FOR LABORERS

Jesus demonstrated a fundamental way to get workers in the church, but we fail so often to apply his teaching. When Jesus saw the crowds as "sheep without a shepherd," he grieved over them with a gut-level compassion (Matthew 9:36). His response, though, was to tell his followers that the problem was not that the fields were not ready for harvest but that there were too few workers (9:37). The answer to this problem was simple: "Ask the Lord of the harvest, therefore, to send out workers into his harvest field" (9:38).

Pray, Jesus instructed, that God would move workers into the field. In fact, the word translated "send out" is a strong word that can be understood as "thrust out." One commentator observes that the word might even refer "to workers already in the field who 'need to have a fire lit under them to thrust them out of their comforts into the world of need.'"[47] Who else but God can light a fire under comfortable believers?

Uninvolved members will not get involved unless God moves their hearts. Enlist a team of current workers, and lead them to pray *by name* for uninvolved members in your church. Pray that God would "thrust them out" into ministry involvement. Then be sure to praise him and thank him when he answers these prayers.

ASK UNINVOLVED MEMBERS WHY THEY AREN'T INVOLVED

This principle seems so simple and logical, but it's often overlooked. We should not assume we know the causes that keep members uninvolved, nor should we strategize to reach these members without first knowing their reasons for uninvolvement. Indeed, sometimes simply asking uninvolved members for their input is a positive step. Just knowing that we view them as important, that we value their opinions, and that their church wants them to be part of the team can be motivating.

Figure 21 provides a brief questionnaire for seeking information from your uninvolved members. The survey challenges members to consider (1) how God used them in the past, (2) the obstacles to involvement they now face, (3) the hobbies or interests that could develop into ministries, and (4) their willingness to talk further about church involvement.

START WITH THE FEW

Imagine this scenario: First Church is located in a growing community, and their pastor is committed to reaching that community. The church currently averages 250 at Sunday morning worship. Church programming includes growing Bible study groups, enthusiastic missions groups, and a strong choir. First Church ought to be a growing church.

But First Church is like many churches, where only a little over one-third of the active adult members volunteer to serve.[48] Many of those who *are* serving are those who have joined the church in the past few years (because the church has raised the bar for newcomers). In this case, though, almost ninety adults are attending but not getting involved.

Frankly, this picture can be overwhelming. How do you make a difference in a church where the majority of adults are uninvolved? One of my pastoral heroes, a longtime pastor named Jack Tichenor, answered this question for me years ago. Drawing on his several decades of pastoral experience, Jack told me, "We're not called to change whole churches. If you try to change the whole church, you'll never get there. We're called to change *lives* rather than churches. Ask God to change a few lives, and the church will

UNINVOLVED MEMBER SURVEY

Ministry Questionnaire

Name: _____ Phone: _____

List any ministry activities or church groups in which you have participated in the past:

_____

_____

_____

List any church positions you held in the past:

_____

_____

_____

Which of the following issues make it difficult for you to serve in your church today? (Please mark all that apply.)

_____ too little time _____ family responsibilities
_____ health issues _____ lack of knowledge about
_____ fear opportunities
_____ personal issues _____ lack of training
_____ other: _____

In general, what hobbies or interests are most important to you?

_____

_____

_____

What can our church do to help you get more involved?

_____

_____

_____

Are you willing to meet with a church leader to discuss opportunities to serve in the church? ____Yes _____ No

Please tell us anything else you want us to know about your church involvement._____

_____

Figure 21

eventually change." These words were spoken by a gentle man who ministered for over sixty years and who saw more than forty young men called to ministry under his pastoral leadership. He understood the profound truth that churches would never change unless individual lives were changed first.

If you want to move your uninvolved members into ministry, don't get caught in the trap of finding the right "program" to make it happen. Do follow the principles listed in this book, but first decide to focus your attention on just a *few* uninvolved members. Ask God to direct you to these members. Then trust his leadership and go after them. Invite them to lunch. Find out why they are not involved. Walk them through the SHAPE or DESIGN process. Make them aware of opportunities for service in your church. Challenge them to get involved. Provide training as needed. And be sure to affirm them when they do get involved.

In a church like First Church, trying to motivate *all* of the uninvolved adults to do ministry is likely going to be a fruitless task. Motivating two or three at a time, though, is indeed possible—and two or three at a time will lead in the end to an involved congregation. Eventually, membership will matter even more in this church.

OTHER SUGGESTIONS FOR MOVING ATTENDERS INTO MEMBERSHIP AND MINISTRY

No research project is really finished when the data is collected and analyzed. Research almost always leads to more discussion, which ideally leads to further insights and greater practical applications. As our team discussed our findings, we found ourselves compiling this list of "other suggestions" we thought could be helpful to church leaders.

TEACH EVANGELISM EARLY

Maybe you recall that 80 percent of the churches we surveyed included the plan of salvation in their membership classes (see table 6, page 65). In fact, some churches used these classes as a part of their primary evangelistic strategy.

Only 42 percent of the churches, however, *intentionally* taught evangelism training in their membership classes (remember, leaders at least modeled evangelism as they shared the gospel, but they often implemented no further training). Most churches that did evangelism training did so in another class, sometimes several months later.

We believe this approach poses a twofold problem. First, believers are usually most passionate about God when they are new believers. I often say that new believers will "tell a wall about Jesus" if that's all they can get to listen. Second, young believers have more access to lost people than most long-term believers do. Young believers are on fire and excited, with a ready-made audience of nonbelievers with whom to disclose how God changed their lives. Why not train them quickly to share their faith? The longer we wait to train them, the more likely they will become insulated in the church.

At a minimum, use your membership class to train new believers to give their testimony according to the outline listed in chapter 4. You can always follow up later with in-depth training, but don't miss this most important first opportunity.

DON'T EXEMPT TRANSFERRING BELIEVERS FROM THE MEMBERSHIP CLASS

When our team began this study, we wondered if we'd find that churches offered different membership classes for young believers and long-term Christians. Surely the needs would be different for those who had recently become Christians compared to those who were only transferring their church membership.

Our research showed, though, that churches did *not* differentiate between these groups. Typically, all new members were expected to attend the same class. Emerson Wiles, pastor of Mililani Baptist

Church in Hawaii, even told one of our researchers, "Billy Graham would be required to take this class if he joined our church."

Essentially, these churches believed *a new member is a new member, regardless of background.* They expected all new members to be believers and to be aware of the church's basic doctrine, vision, and expectations. As Mark, a lay leader in a Wisconsin Evangelical Free church told us, "Giving the same basic information to all new members will get everyone on the same page, regardless of their spiritual backgrounds."

Indeed, some of the long-term believers we interviewed were attending their first membership class—and it didn't matter how many churches they had previously joined. Doris, for example, had been a Christian for forty years before she voluntarily attended her first membership class at her Tennessee church. As she completed the class, she said she now "had a clearer understanding of what the Bible says about my role as a Christian, about the expectations God has of me."

Churches did at times differentiate between new believers and long-term believers in their follow-up classes. For example, new believers may go on to take basic Bible study courses, while long-term believers may attend in-depth classes. When it came to membership, though, both groups attended together.

MAKE A COMMITMENT TO EVALUATE YOUR MEMBERSHIP CLASS CONSISTENTLY

I teach at what I believe is the greatest seminary in the world— The Southern Baptist Theological Seminary in Louisville, Kentucky. My colleagues are some of the most brilliant believers I've ever met. Many have decades of teaching experience. Still, our administration requires us to do course evaluations at the end of every semester. There's always room for improvement, and our administrators expect us to keep pushing for excellence in the classroom.

I wish I could report that the churches we studied were equally diligent in evaluating their membership classes. But only twelve of the fifty-two churches in our study (23 percent) included evaluation at the end of the class—and most did so only informally. Time and again, survey respondents told us they gained feedback about the class by "just asking class members how they liked the class."

The churches that formally evaluated these classes typically provided a brief questionnaire critiquing the course content and schedule. One church, Carlisle Baptist Church in Panama City, Florida, formally evaluated the new member's overall experience (beyond just the membership class). We've adapted this form and provided it as a sample evaluation form in appendix 12.

DON'T FORGET THE CHILDREN AND YOUTH

Let's hear a little more from Doris, the forty-year Christian. When we asked her if the membership class should be *required*, she answered in the affirmative: "The new member class is very helpful because as a new Christian, you do not know very much about the Christian life or church membership. I feel it helps any new member and new Christian to learn more about the Bible and the church. Also, this class is very helpful to long-term members who have never had this training, as *I never did in the small church where I was raised* [emphasis added]."

Take a moment to read that last line again. Forty years after becoming a Christian, Doris finally received some basic training! While we can only guess at the answer, would her Christian walk have been different had she received training when she was a new believer?

Our research at the Billy Graham School has shown that 83 percent of the people who become Christians do so before the age of twenty.[49] If so, it is imperative that churches be prepared to train children and youth when they first become believers.

Our research project focused on adult membership classes, but we also heard about children's new believer classes in the course of our study. We challenge churches to be prepared to train the youngest believers God gives to their congregations. Two important resources to help meet this challenge are *Survival Kit for New Christians: Children's Edition* and *I'm a Christian Now!*[50]

THE PEG GAME

In the introduction to this chapter you learned that I don't like jigsaw puzzles. There is, however, one type of puzzle I *do* like—the "Peg Game." If you've been inside a Cracker Barrel restaurant, you've probably seen this puzzle on every table. The object is to jump individual pegs, leaving just one peg in its hole at the end of the game. During my many visits to Cracker Barrel, I've spent hours jumping pegs, never willing to give up until I get it right.

I hope you have this same kind of enthusiasm as you lead your church to move attenders into membership and ministry. You may need to jump one peg at a time, and you may have to rethink your strategy occasionally—but don't give up. In the next chapter, you will hear from pastors whose stories will encourage you to make membership matter in your congregation.

HELPFUL APPENDIXES

Appendix 11: Sample Sermon Outline
Appendix 12: New Member Evaluation Form

QUESTIONS FOR CONSIDERATION

1. If your church has a membership class, have most of the church's leaders taken the course? If not, what plans do you have to teach them the course material?
2. Who are the prayer warriors you'll enlist to join you in praying for laborers?

3. Who are the uninvolved members you'll personally contact and lead toward involvement?
4. After reading this chapter, what one change or improvement might you make in your church's membership class?

Chapter 8

"Just Give Me the Facts"

A Pastors' Forum

———— ❧ ————

As a young pastor, I read as many books and attended as many conferences as I could in order to learn how to lead a church. I learned the most, though, by listening to other church leaders who had led, or who were effectively leading, their own churches. The goal of this chapter is to let you listen to leaders of churches that move attenders into membership and ministry. Six pastors agreed to contribute to this discussion (table 10).[51]

Each of these men responded to five questions posed by our research team. We'll let them speak for themselves in this chapter, trusting that you will learn much from them.

Question 1: Explain your church's membership process, i.e., how does one become a member of your church?

KH: You become a member of Valley View by committing your life to Jesus and following through with baptism or by your testimony that you have previously done so. We still have a walk-forward invitation, but we do not present the people at that time. We simply celebrate with those making decisions, which allows us time to counsel strategically with those who have come forward.

CONTRIBUTING PASTORS AND THEIR CHURCHES			
Church	**Location**	**Pastor**	**Growth**
Valley View	Louisville, Kentucky	Kevin Hamm (KH)	From 300 to 2,000+ in seven years
Sandia Presbyterian	Albuquerque, New Mexico	Dewey Johnson (DJ)	From 6 in 1990 to 760+ today
Valley Baptist	Bakersfield, California	Roger Spradlin (RS)	Averaging 2,280 in 2000; 2,900 in worship and 2,500 in Sunday school in 2004
Harpeth Community	Franklin, Tennessee	Bob Harrington (BH)	Averaging 275 in 2000; 470 in 2004
Chapel Hill Presbyterian	Gig Harbor, Washington	Stuart Bond (SB)	Averaging 1,187 in 2000; 1,700 in 2004
Hunter Street Baptist	Birmingham, Alabama	Buddy Gray (BG)	Averaging 2,900 in 2000; 3,550 in 2004

Table 10

You can also become a member at the conclusion of our "Discovery Class," which discusses our purpose, vision, and so forth.

DJ: In the Presbyterian Church, a candidate for membership appears before the governing board (session) and gives one of the responses listed below. We encourage all potential candidates to attend our inquiry class before meeting with the session.

- If the person has never made a profession of faith and been baptized, he or she responds affirmatively to the question "Do you affirm your faith in Jesus Christ as Lord and Savior, and will you be a faithful member of this congregation, giving of yourself as God has equipped you for Christ's service?" A time of baptism is then arranged.

- If the person is a member in good standing of another congregation, he or she simply requests that a letter of membership transfer be sent to our church.
- If the person has made a profession of faith and been baptized but a letter of membership transfer is not forthcoming, he or she makes a reaffirmation of faith.

RS: People join our church through baptism by immersion following conversion, through transfer of membership from a church of like faith and order, or by statement of their faith and Christian baptism. Regarding church membership, our church constitution also states:

- Following counseling to confirm that the candidate is qualified for membership according to the church constitution, the candidate will be presented in a church service for affirmation by the members. Individuals who are living in open adultery or fornication or are engaging in homosexual behavior are ineligible for membership.
- All new members of this church will be asked to participate in the new member orientation process. In addition, the new believer will be asked to complete a study of basic Christian disciplines.

We have an invitation at the end of every worship service. People are invited to join our church and to make other spiritual commitments as well. When a person comes forward, he or she is greeted by one of our pastors. Children are directed to one of our children's ministry staff members. Individuals are briefly counseled at the front of the church before being introduced to the congregation at the end of the service. During the closing prayer, they are then led to a private area to be individually counseled by a pastor.

At this initial meeting, they are instructed regarding baptism or questioned regarding their baptism. They are given a membership covenant and invited to the next membership information meeting. New believers are invited to a class designed for them. Children are required to read and fill out a special booklet before they can be baptized. After completing the booklet, they must meet with someone from the children's ministry team for an interview. Children must be nine years old before they are baptized.

BH: People first connect with Harpeth Community Church through one of our groups or through the Sunday morning worship service. Those who first connect through a small group eventually attend the Sunday morning service, which becomes the place of primary contact. Those who fill in "prayer and care" cards are contacted and invited to our 101 seminar. The purpose of this seminar, advertised every week in our bulletin, is "to explain the core teachings in the Bible on what it is to be a Christian." Then, after the 101 seminar, if people continue to attend church, they are invited to our 201 seminar, which explains the beliefs, mission, vision, values, and programs of the church. At the end of 201, people are invited to make a commitment to become members.

SB: To become a member you need to go through our class. We have five of these a year. Three are a full weekend (Friday night, Saturday 9:00 a.m. to 5:00 p.m.). Two are a pair of sequential Sunday afternoons. At the end of the class, we will have gone over their personal relationship with Jesus Christ, some theological foundations, what it means to be a Presbyterian, and the responsibilities of membership.

During the class they will have met three times in small groups and are invited/expected to become part of an ongoing small group. At the end of the class, they need to deal with four membership questions:

- Who is your Lord and Savior?
- Do you trust in him?
- Do you intend to be his disciple, to obey his word, and to show his love?
- Will you be a faithful member of this congregation, giving of yourselves in every way, and will you seek the fellowship of the church wherever you may be?

BG: People are accepted into the Hunter Street church family by receiving Jesus Christ as Savior and Lord and obeying him through believers' baptism by immersion; by transfer of membership from another Baptist church (having already made a profession of faith in Christ and having been baptized by immersion); by statement of faith in Jesus Christ, with prior membership in a church that teaches salvation through Jesus Christ, then obedience through believers' baptism; or by baptism from another Christian denomination, having made a profession of faith in Jesus Christ but having never been baptized by immersion as a believer.

We offer a monthly membership information class. This class helps attenders make an informed decision in their personal commitment to Christ and to our church family. The class may be attended by anyone desiring information, but it is also a requirement for church membership. When requesting membership, attenders complete a commitment card that includes our membership covenant, to which they signify agreement by their signature. People may present themselves for membership at the close of a worship service and then attend the membership information class, or they may attend the class and join at the close of the class.

Question 2: Some say that people don't want to join churches today. Have you found this to be the case? How does your church emphasize membership?

KH: If people are anxious about joining a church, it's usually because they don't know what we expect of them. In other words, they don't know *how to join* the church—so I try to briefly explain this process each Sunday during the response time. We also have a "New Members' Board" in the lobby, which allows our people to see the new members' pictures while emphasizing the positive aspects of being a church member. The names of the new members are also listed in our Sunday and Wednesday bulletins in order to emphasize the importance of church membership and to allow our people to celebrate what God is doing in the lives of people and in the church.

DJ: Some persons join rather soon, but others take longer. But Sandia Presbyterian Church has not encountered a nonjoining attitude, other than in a small portion of our worshipers. We constantly emphasize membership. Pictures of our newest members are posted prominently by the doors leading into the sanctuary. New members are introduced monthly to the congregation in a worship service. And new member dinners are held quarterly at the senior pastor's home.

To make candidates for membership aware of the inquiry meetings and the next session meeting, a standard procedure is followed week after week, month after month:

- During the "ritual of friendship" time at every worship service, the senior or associate pastor says, "For those of you looking for a church home, our next inquiry class at Sandia Presbyterian Church will be held on _____. Please sign up on the sheet in the fellowship hall."
- "Blurbs" promoting the inquiry class are in every issue of the newsletter and every Sunday morning bulletin.
- A first-time visitor receives a letter of welcome from the senior pastor, along with a brochure about all the available programs and ministries. A second-time visitor gets a phone call from the new member coordinator. A third-time visitor gets another letter from the senior pastor, inviting him or her to an inquiry class.

RS: An attitude of not wanting to join may be more prevalent in places like California, where people may not be as likely to have a church heritage. We emphasize the importance of church membership in our membership information class. We have a saying: "We want people to not only believe but belong." Also, I mention in my sermons the importance of membership with regard to areas of accountability and ministry involvement. We talk of the church as a family to which we belong.

A person cannot serve in a ministry position in our church unless he or she is a member and has signed the leadership covenant. Therefore, membership means something at Valley Baptist. It represents connection, belonging, family, and accountability.

BH: Most eventually want to join the church. However, we have found that those who don't want to financially support the church or who don't want further involvement (beyond attending the main worship service) will not attend our 201 seminar or, if they have attended it, will not become members. We invite all regular attenders to become members, and we emphasize that it is an important part of discipleship and growth in one's spiritual journey.

With new Christians, we've found that they need time before they will commit to membership. Because we have two seminars before membership, it allows time for them to process what it means to be a Christian and then to discover who we are and our expectations of them as a church. If membership is pushed quickly, especially with high expectations, many find we are asking for too much too fast. We look at both conversion and membership as the fruit of a process, and we want to be careful not to rush people.

SB: Yes, it is true that membership is suspect. People enter church with one hand on the door and the other guarding their wallet. Membership means "I'm diving in." It's not unusual for people in our church to have attended for over a year before they join. We try to fight this by announcing the membership classes, providing testimonies from people who have attended, and showing videos of the class. We want people to see that this is a compelling, life-impacting experience.

We've recently adopted a new approach that emphasizes membership. After the new members answer their membership questions before the congregation, we ask all members to stand and recite, along with the new members, these promises of membership:

- Gather—I promise to worship at Chapel Hill regularly and to share my life with others in this church family.
- Glorify—I promise to love God with all my heart.
- Grapple—I promise to wrestle with life's challenges while holding on to Jesus.
- Give—I promise to be obedient to God's claim on my money and my talents for his work at Chapel Hill.
- Go—I promise to stretch myself to reach others with God's love and truth.

This approach runs the risk of alienating nonmembers, but we think the greater opportunity is that it elevates membership in a way that invites others to join.

BG: People are more noncommittal than ever before, so teaching the importance of commitment is crucial to the spiritual life of an individual and of the church corporately. The percentage of "regular attenders" has risen slightly over the past decade but not significantly here at Hunter Street. Church membership is a requirement for all lay leadership positions at our church.

Membership in God's family is emphasized by teaching the biblical foundation for church membership from the pulpit and in Sunday morning Bible study classes. Information on "How to Join the Church Family" is printed in the weekly Sunday morning worship bulletins. Once a month in the worship bulletin worshipers are encouraged to register for the membership information class. I also write a letter to all guests who worship with us for the third time, extending an invitation to attend the membership information class.

Each month prior to the class, the membership minister then personally invites all who have expressed an interest in the membership information class or who have been regularly attending worship. "Membership leaders" of Sunday morning Bible study classes also promote the membership information class to attenders who have not yet joined the church. We have found that our church members are the best encouragers for church membership, as they share their enthusiasm for being part of our church family.

Question 3: How does your church move people from membership into ministry? How do you get them involved?

KH: We have a simple four-step process for assimilation. We show this process on the worship center screen just about every Sunday, so people know what we are going to ask them:

- *Step #1*: Attend the "Member Information Class"—a one-time, sixty-minute class we offer every month. This class acquaints the new member with everything we have to offer. We've put together a little notebook that lets them know about every ministry at Valley View. Those who want to join are also required to sign a membership covenant at the end of this class, which is another way to communicate our expectations of them and our commitment to them.
- *Step #2*: Join a small group. At the end of the member information class, we encourage participants to join a small group, which involves a Sunday morning Bible fellowship class and possibly a monthly care group.
- *Step #3*: Attend the "Pastor's Discovery Class"—a three-hour class we offer every other month on a Sunday afternoon. This class discusses our vision, doctrine, mission, and so forth. We also require this class for every leader in our church.
- *Step #4*: Attend the "Servants by Design Class"—a three-hour class we offer every other Sunday afternoon at the same time as the discovery class. This class looks at personalities,

spiritual gifts, and opportunities to serve. We are constantly encouraging our people to invite others to serve with them in areas of their passion.

DJ: Sandia Presbyterian Church has from its beginning been blessed with about 20 percent of the attenders of each worship service being nonmembers. We've always welcomed nonmembers to join in our programs or ministries—to test the fit and to try out what it would feel like to be a member. The only things a nonmember cannot do are cast a vote in a congregational meeting and serve as an officer.

Informally, staff members and church members are always urging other members to get involved. Our formal process of moving people into ministry includes the following:

- During our basic discipleship courses, we invite participants to go one step further and take our SHAPE course, discover their gifts, and find their ministry niche.
- During our three-hour inquiry class, I promote our seven core commitments, one of which is "find your ministry."[52] We describe our programs and ministries, including the SHAPE class.
- Our annual commitment card is also distributed and discussed during the inquiry class. This large card (8 ×13) outlines for new member candidates how we expect our members to get involved: Pray for Sandia _____ times per month; attend worship _____ times per month; attend Bible study/Sunday school/small group _____ times per month; invite _____ persons to church functions in [current year]; serve in Christ's church as indicated below, and then we list various volunteer opportunities the candidate can choose.
- New members are received at the monthly session meeting and then dismissed to discuss with the new member coordinator, the volunteer coordinator, and the associate pastor

how they are going to get involved. The volunteer coordinator keeps a data bank of volunteer information.

- The commitment card is distributed to all members and updated during stewardship season each year. The commitment to a volunteer ministry runs from February of one year through January of the next. We devote time each January to train volunteers for their ministries.

RS: At our membership information dinner, we survey new members' ministry experience and interests. This information is passed on to the appropriate ministry leader. The ministry leader will then interview and personally recruit new members for ministry if they are needed and are ready to serve.

In our discipleship ministry we have a system for developing leaders called LIFE—"Leadership Institute for Equipping." The classes generally meet for an hour and a half for thirteen weeks, and we offer classes on four levels. The first level includes foundational classes for Christian living. The second level includes classes that are foundational for ministry. The third level consists of general leadership and communication classes. The fourth level includes ministry-specific classes; for example, there are child development classes for those who work with children, music classes for those who want to be part of a music ministry, and youth worker classes. A person is certified as a leader after so many classes have been taken in each level.

Each May we have a "leadership fast track" that lasts four weeks. The first week's class focuses on general leadership principles. At the other weeks' classes, various ministry leaders explain their specific ministry and the opportunities for service. Interested individuals then come alongside a ministry leader in a ministry context for three weeks in order to determine if they want to pursue that particular ministry.

BH: Those who become members commit "to do their best to be actively involved in an area of service at Harpeth Community

Church." We set ministry as a key part of membership. Then, after our membership seminar (201), we strongly encourage members to attend our 301 seminar. The purpose of this seminar is to help people identify their spiritual gifts; in the process, we help people see how they might uniquely serve in certain areas. We set up a special one-on-one interview with a staff member, who helps find the best place of service to match each person's giftedness. We've found that shoulder tapping, where we personally as leaders ask for their specific help in a ministry, is the key to getting people involved.

SB: First, many people become involved at some level before they become members. Second, our specific strategy for getting them involved at a personal level is the follow-up small groups. In this setting, they gain the relational strength to try something new. Third, at the time of each inquiry class we also create a "getting connected" list of the current jobs that are available. We do find, though, that we're not as effective as we wish we were in this regard. We need more follow-up and more connecting of people to ministries.

BG: "Every member is a minister" is practiced by the ministerial staff through equipping the saints to do the work of ministry and also by members as they become educated to realize they are ministers as well.

Sunday morning Bible study classes are fundamental to the goal of seeing our members become involved in the life of our church. It is here that people grow together in Bible study, personal relationships, and ministry to guests and members alike. Every person who joins our church family is assigned to be a member of a Bible study class. Many of those who join our church have already been attending a class. They are assigned as potential members to classes immediately following their first worship visit. These classes are responsible for ongoing contact under the guidance of the class "membership leader."

Because we believe church health is more important than church growth, the goal of becoming a "grand slam disciple" is promoted throughout the church body. Once people commit to church membership, they attend our "second base" discipleship class, where they learn the basics of how to begin maturing in their walk with Christ. After that, they attend the "third base" class. Each potential class attendee completes a questionnaire defining his or her "SHAPE." The class includes a ministry fair, where attenders can visit exhibits of all the church ministries in which they can be involved. Those indicating interest in a ministry are contacted by the minister of that particular area and then trained for service. Different ministries are spotlighted in weekly and monthly publications, with testimonies and invitations for people to become involved.

Question 4: What is the value of your church's membership class? What is your role in the class?

KH: The entire membership process has been critical to helping us sustain our growth. Emphasizing the importance of membership has helped us keep a close eye on the back door of the church. We certainly aren't perfect in this area, but we are much, much improved since implementing our assimilation strategy. I lead the discovery class, and I also emphasize the four-step assimilation strategy from the pulpit.

DJ: Our class is called the "Inquiry Class into Sandia Presbyterian Church." It consists almost entirely of nonmembers who want to know what belonging to SPC entails. I personally conduct this class in my capacity as senior pastor. It gives me the opportunity to get to know newcomers—and they get to know me. This personal touch helps me pick up on some things right away—baptisms to be performed, kids to be channeled into youth group, obvious interests and gifts, and so forth.

Among the many other benefits, this class gives me an opportunity to go over denominational history, to share the history and structure of Sandia Presbyterian Church, to define church membership and explain the benefits thereof, to go over the core commitments of

Sandia—what we expect of members—and to promote our hands-on missions and mission giving, both locally and globally.

RS: We have a membership class that meets each month on Sunday evening. We call it a membership information meeting because anyone who is interested in becoming a member may attend, as may the new member. Generally between thirty and eighty people attend. The meeting is divided into three parts. My co-pastor leads the first part, which covers the church's confession of faith and doctrinal distinctives. I take over for the next hour, dealing first with our church government and structure. I also talk about our church's strategy, which includes a discussion of our ministry philosophy and vision. Our minister of discipleship concludes with a third session about our opportunities for service. During this time he talks about ministry and ways to get involved.

It's been our experience that families will often join our church immediately after attending the information class. Also, I've found that those who attend feel more personally connected to me as their pastor.

We also have a new believers class that meets during Sunday school. The class is four weeks long and runs continually. A new believer can start at any point. We have a group of people called "encouragers" who are assigned to new believers to help them in one-on-one discipleship.

BH: The value of the classes (we do two seminars) is very high. You cannot become a member without attending both of them. We have also found that people really value and appreciate the two classes after they've attended them because it has helped them to know where the church stands and what it believes.

I teach the first seminar ("Christian Basics") because my gifting is evangelism, because people want to get to know the lead pastor, and because I want to make an early connection with everyone who will become a member. I share the second seminar (the beliefs, mission, vision, values, and practices of the church) with my associate minister.

SB: The value of a membership class is that it acculturates people to our church. It says that our values are Jesus, relationships, excellence, honesty, and the journey of faith. In addition, we are able to see from our data that membership means "buy in" for individuals. They realize this is their church and they need to support it financially.

Several features make our class so important:

- *Our pastors make it a priority.* We make sure we are in town to teach the classes. We tell our stories, and by the end of the class, most people have the sense they know us far better than they had expected. We keep it positive, relational, and from the heart. We are real and personable throughout.

- *The gospel is preached in a clear, relational way.* If you are not a Christian, it's a very supportive and compelling environment in which to make the commitment. The people tell their own stories. The last small group is where they share their prepared statement of their own faith stories. There is nothing more powerful than this. Such stories are typically accompanied by tears and hugs.

- *The behind-the-scenes work of the leaders is tremendous.* They meet after each small group, process what is happening in their groups, and direct one another to move effectively with the problem talkers and the spiritual neophytes.

- *We "put on the dog."* We provide snacks for class members, and it's obvious to the new members that this is a very high value for us. Name tags are premade, accommodations for those with disabilities are taken into consideration, and child care is provided at all times. It is a big deal, and they know it.

BG: As pastor, my role is to teach the class and personally interact with the attenders. Membership information class attenders hear the plan of salvation and have an opportunity to respond; receive detailed information about our purpose statement, strategy, and structure as a church; understand what is expected of them as members of our church family and what they can expect of their church family; meet other newcomers to the church; and personally connect with the pastor. They are encouraged to make a commitment to Christ and the church.

Question 5. What practical advice can you give to pastors who want to raise the membership standards and expectations in their churches?

KH: I'd suggest that pastors connect with other churches that are already doing a decent job in this area. I'd also mention that you cannot overemphasize the need for the pastor to be vocally supportive and positive about membership and assimilation changes and requirements.

DJ: Adopt something like Sandia's "seven core commitments"—you can call them the "five whatevers" or the "six something elses." Yet, what it does is lay out in a memorable form what the congregation expects of its members. Enumerating the expectations hardly wins the day, but at least it's a start. From then on you have to keep these in front of the congregation and build on them.

Because SPC allows nonmembers to participate in our programs and ministries, I tell my inquiry class that we will take care of them as long as they like without joining—*but* when they join, they make a full commitment to the work of Jesus Christ in and through Sandia. This way *membership* is further linked with the word *commitment*.

RS: I believe two things are essential in raising the membership bar. One is a *membership covenant* that clearly spells out what is expected of a member. I go over this covenant in our member information meeting. The second essential is a *membership class*. It doesn't have to be required if it is clearly expected and done well. A lot of information can be communicated in a short time. Members will only value membership if they are taught to value it. You cannot raise membership expectations without having a mechanism to communicate these standards. The membership covenant and the membership class are the two best mechanisms I know of for such communication.

BH: I'm a big advocate of membership classes, membership covenants, and membership expectations. The class is a no-brainer. Why would you have people as members who do not know what the church believes and where it is going? What better process to help people understand these matters than a membership class or classes?

Membership covenants (when properly done) are very healthy. They establish up front the basis of the relationship between church leaders and members. Members are formally taught the things they need for a healthy spiritual life and the commitments and practices that are necessary for their spiritual growth.

Membership expectations are very important as long as they are healthy ones. We ask everyone who becomes a member to commit to the "Three S's"—Sunday morning worship, a small group, and an area of service. We ask people to commit "to do their best" to become regularly involved in these groups (note that it is important to avoid absolutistic language).

SB: First, *don't be afraid of taking on this issue*. It is vitally important that you set the standard for what you want. A poorly planned or executed class says this whole experience isn't really very important. Second, *get your elders and leaders involved*. Make sure they are part of the process as facilitators. Third, *commit your time and resources*. It will be one of the best returns on investment in ministry you can experience.

BG: Share your vision with the church (create a sense of destiny), and "plow the ground" with your core members regarding any change. Change the easiest thing first. In addition, don't take criticism personally when it comes. Be willing to let people leave the church if they don't agree with the church's direction. More than anything else, *pray* as you make these changes!

LEARNING FROM THESE CHURCHES

By this point in this book, you may have been expecting similarities in the stories of these church leaders. These pastors believe that membership matters, and they've led their churches to believe the same thing. They preach membership, publicize membership classes, and promote opportunities for ministry and service.

Their plans for moving members into ministry are both proactive and preventive. They *expect* members to get involved and tell them so. Strategic follow-up and accountability through small groups help prevent spectator church members. The point is, these churches have intentional strategies in place to move attenders into membership and members into ministry. None claim to be perfect and all see room for improvement, but they are (in Kevin Hamm's words) "already doing a decent job in this area."

Perhaps your church can learn from what they are doing. Even one insight properly applied in your particular context will be a step in the right direction.

QUESTIONS FOR CONSIDERATION

1. According to these pastors, how important is it that church leaders continually emphasize membership and ministry?
2. What role do small groups play in the membership and ministry placement processes in these churches? How do the small groups in your church contribute to these processes?
3. Buddy Gray encouraged leaders to be "willing to let people leave the church if they don't agree with the church's direction." How do you respond to this statement?
4. After reading this chapter, what one change or improvement might you make in your church's membership class?

Chapter 9

TIM'S STORY

I n my book *Discipled Warriors*, I tell the story of Tim, who became a believer at the age of twenty when a friend told him about God's saving grace.[53] He rapidly became a fervent evangelist, telling everyone he knew (and sometimes those he didn't know) about Jesus. Few people served God with the kind of passion Tim had.

Indeed, his church leaders quickly recognized Tim's leadership potential, and they asked him to teach a Bible study class. As you might expect, Tim carried out the task with zeal. His class began to set the example for outreach and growth in this church.

What no one but Tim knew, though, was that he was struggling in his Christian walk. He read the Scriptures only sporadically—and most often only to prepare to teach his next lesson. Prayer was difficult. Failure in temptation was common. Even his fire for personal evangelism began to wane. In essence, Tim was a defeated believer who was still carrying out a leadership role in his church.

The problem for Tim, however, wasn't that he did not want to be faithful to God. He genuinely wanted to know God's Word and apply it properly in his life. He desired to be a prayer warrior like others he heard about in his church. As much as anything, he hungered for a renewal of his evangelistic passion.

Tim's problem was that he really did not know *how* to initiate and maintain these spiritual disciplines—because *no one in his church had ever taught him.* His church told him to read the Word, but no one showed him how. They told him to "pray without ceasing" but didn't teach him what the phrase meant. Nobody taught him how to face and overcome temptation. Leaders encouraged him to "keep up the good work" in witnessing, but they failed to help him overcome discouragement when others didn't respond. Yet the same leaders put Tim in a position of spiritual leadership, with the responsibility of teaching others the Word of God.

To put it simply, Tim's church failed him. They reached him but then did little to disciple him. At the same time, though, they made Tim a teacher. The result? Tim was on the front lines of ministry without being equipped with the personal disciplines to fight the daily battles.

THE PROBLEM: NO DISCIPLING STRATEGY

Tim's story is important to me for two reasons. First and foremost, his story is strikingly similar to mine. I am grateful for that associate pastor who involved me in the bus ministry and the Sunday school director who allowed me to teach a class, but how I longed as a young believer for someone to give me more specific, personal guidance! How badly I wanted to sit at somebody's feet and learn, much like the disciples did at the feet of Jesus. Regrettably, I did not have that opportunity until almost seven years into my Christian life.

In addition, Tim's story is one I hear again and again wherever I travel. Anecdotally, about 75 percent of the persons who attend the conferences I lead tell a similar story. These are evangelicals, committed to Christ and his Word—but they've never been discipled. Their hunger to learn is often overwhelming, and their disappointment in never having been taught is obvious.

Today, I am driven by a desire to address this problem. Two of my books, *Discipled Warriors* and *Making Disciples through Mentoring*,[54] address this concern directly. My prayer is that the book you now hold in your hands will help confront this issue as well.

MAKING MEMBERSHIP MATTER THROUGH DISCIPLE MAKING

I fear that some leaders will take a few steps in the right direction after reading this book but then stop short. They will implement a membership class and begin a ministry placement strategy without doing both within the context of an *overall* disciple-making plan. They will make a start but have no final goal in mind.

To be fair, many of the churches we studied were at least working toward a disciple-making strategy. My concern is that some readers may, in their enthusiasm to raise the membership bar, miss this point. For that reason, I close this book with a final challenge: *As you make membership matter in your church, develop a clear disciple-making strategy.* Don't stop with a membership class and a ministry placement strategy. Two simple guidelines will help you keep disciple making in the forefront.

DECIDE WHAT "DISCIPLED DAVE" LOOKS LIKE

Suppose Dave were to join your church next Sunday as a new believer. He has no church background, and he lacks basic knowledge about the Christian walk. All he knows is that God transformed his life.

Assume that Dave remains as a member of your church for the next three or four years. At the end of that time, what do you want him to be? That is, what should this baby Christian look like several years later? No believer is ever fully discipled in this world—we always have room for growth—but this description can give your church a goal to aim for. Your goal should be to produce "Discipled Dave."

Jesus' teachings ought to guide us here. His disciples must be willing to forsake all, take up their cross, and follow him (Luke 14:26–27, 33). They must continue in his word (John 8:31–32), obeying his commands (John 14:15). Their love for each other and the fruit of their Christian life will show that they are his followers (John 13:35; 15:8).

The apostle Paul's writings, too, help us. Believers are to live worthy of their calling (Ephesians 4:1), exhibiting the fruit of the Spirit (Galatians 5:22). They are to have the servant-humility of Christ (Philippians 2:5–7). The "new self" is to be evident in their lives (Colossians 3:1–13). Equipped members are to do ministry, building up the church in the process (Ephesians 4:11–12). In essence, believers are to be imitators of God (Ephesians 5:1) as God conforms them to the image of his Son (Romans 8:29). "Discipled Dave" should increasingly live like Jesus.

Figure 22 gives you a model of what Discipled Dave might look like. The goal of this approach is to provide some specific markers by which we might evaluate Dave's Christian growth through his local church. Your model may include other components, but it's important to at least have a goal in mind. A beginning strategy with no goal won't take you very far.

DEVELOP A PLAN, AND MENTOR SOMEBODY IN THE MEANTIME

The next question, of course, is "Does your church have a plan to help Discipled Dave become what you want him to be?" If not, a membership class is a place to begin—but not end. Beyond that, patiently develop the strategy. Provide Christian education that includes basic doctrinal teachings, Bible interpretation, and apologetics. Build a small group system that includes spiritual discipline training and accountability. Promote ministry opportunities, and offer training for each specific ministry. Plan evangelism training sessions, followed by evangelistic and missions opportunities to put the training into practice.

Then establish a plan to monitor members' growth. A church that provides a system of disciple making has a right to hold members accountable for their discipleship. Appendix 13 provides a checklist that may serve as a model for evaluating Discipled Dave's spiritual growth in any particular area of the Christian life.

DISCIPLED DAVE

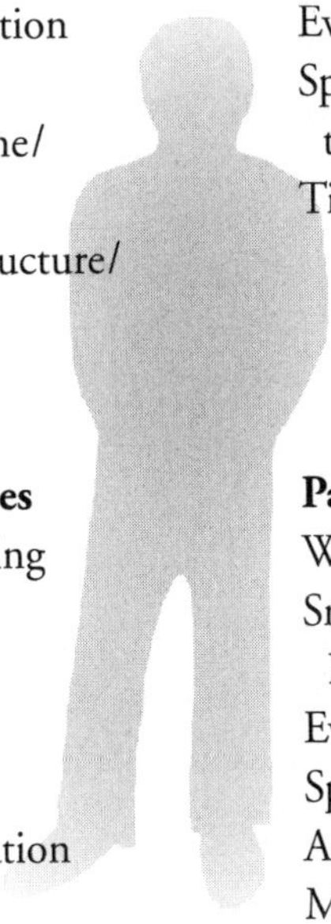

Knowledge
Basic Bible organization
Plan of salvation
Basic church doctrine/
  structure
Denominational structure/
  polity
Hermeneutics

Ministry Skills
Evangelism
Specific ministry
  training
Time management

Spiritual Disciplines
Bible study/journaling
Prayer and fasting
Giving/stewardship
Service
Evangelism
Scripture memorization

Participation
Worship services
Small group/
  Bible study
Evangelism training
Specific ministry service
Accountability group
Missions trip

Theology
Understanding basic beliefs
Defending the faith
  apologetically

Lifestyle
Forsaking sin patterns
Handling temptation
Building healthy
  relations
Exhibiting the new self

Figure 22

Yet, even as I write these words, I know some readers are thinking, "Doing all of this stuff will take a long time!" Indeed, a thorough process will take some time to develop, though you can build on small groups and ministries already in place in your church.

Invest in your current ministry, put the puzzle together one piece at a time, and commit to doing what it takes to produce Discipled Dave.

In the meantime, however, don't put off disciple making until your church process is complete. If you wait for all of the infrastructure to be in place, you may never begin. Instead, start today by mentoring a couple of believers. Just as we suggested that you begin with the *few* when motivating uninvolved members, make membership matter *one life at a time* while you are moving everything else into place. Pour yourself into the lives of one or two potential Discipled Daves—believers who may just be waiting for someone to help them grow in Christ.

Do what Jesus did. Pray for wisdom in selecting some believers to mentor. Teach them the basics. Walk alongside them, modeling faith. Pray *for* them and *with* them. Equip them to evangelize, and send them out to try their skills. Give them permission to ask you questions. Patiently yet firmly guide them through their questions. Hold them accountable to righteous living. Show them how to live as Christ did—and perhaps even how to die. In the end, your church will be stronger, even while you are putting into place a membership and ministry placement strategy.

Remember Tim? Though his church had no functioning discipling plan when he first joined, a caring Christian brother eventually began to mentor him. By the time his church developed a disciple-making strategy, Tim was legitimately ready to lead the way.

Lead your church to develop your own strategy, but don't miss the Tims along the way. Membership matters, because individual members matter.

HELPFUL APPENDIXES

Appendix 13: Spiritual Growth Checklist

QUESTIONS FOR CONSIDERATION

1. Is your story like Tim's story? Why or why not?
2. What would Discipled Dave look like in your church?
3. Who are the believers in your church you could mentor?
4. What obstacles may be standing in the way of your serving as a mentor? How will you overcome them?

SAMPLE INVITATION LETTER

adapted from the one used by Valley View Church,
Louisville, Kentucky

Dear _____,

Again, we want to welcome you to our church. For most people, joining a church can be overwhelming and somewhat confusing in knowing how to get involved. We want to encourage your involvement by providing answers to all of your questions. Your first step is to attend the new member orientation class. Here is what will happen in this class:

- Video clip of ministries/welcome from pastor
- Free Wednesday dinner meal pass
- Printed church directory
- Overview of ministries
- Tour of facilities
- Welcome bag
- Question and answer time

This is a onetime, sixty-minute class that will be offered *every Sunday*. I want to encourage you to attend the 9:00 worship service, then join us at 10:45 for the orientation class. We designed this class especially for you as a new member. Children will be in Bible Fellowship.

---

continued on next page . . .

Date: _____

Time: 10:45 a.m.

Location: Fellowship Hall

Leader: _____

I plan to see you this Sunday. I am looking forward to meeting you personally. Feel free to call with any questions. We are so glad you are here!

God bless,

_____

Director, New Member Involvement

Phone: _____

"Getting to Know You" Form 1

adapted from the one used by Living Hope Baptist Church,
Bowling Green, Kentucky

Getting to Know You

Today's date: _____

Name: _____

Birthday: _____/_____/_____

Address: _____

_____

Phone #: _____ Email: _____

Family Information

Spouse's Name: _____

　　Birthday: ___/___/___

Child's Name: _____

　　Birthday: ___/___/___

Child's Name: _____

　　Birthday: ___/___/___

Child's Name: _____

　　Birthday: ___/___/___

Child's Name: _____

　　Birthday: ___/___/___

Salvation, Baptism, and Membership (please check all that apply)

❑ I have asked Jesus to come into my life. I became a Christian at the age of _____.

❑ I am still considering a relationship with Jesus Christ. I have not yet become a Christian.

❑ I have been baptized by immersion since becoming a Christian.

❑ I have not been baptized but would like the church to contact me to schedule a baptism.

❑ I am moving my membership from the following church (list name, city, and state):

_____

_____

Growing and Serving (please check all that apply)

❑ I am already in a small group led by _____.

❑ I am not in a small group but would like more information about being in one.

❑ I am already in an Adult Bible Fellowship (ABF) led by

_____.

❑ I am not in an ABF but would like more information about being in one.

❑ I am already serving in the following ministry/ministries:

_____

_____

_____

❑ I would rather be serving in the following areas(s):

_____

_____

_____

_____

Appendix 3

"Getting to Know You" Form 2

adapted from Peoples Church, Fresno, California

Part 1: Getting to Know You

Name: _____

Address: _____

City: _____

State: _____ Zip: _____

Phone: (H) _____

Phone: (W) _____

Email: _____

> Picture here

We'd like to get to know you better. Please share with us what you feel comfortable telling us about yourself, your family, and your work.

Your age group (circle)

18 to 23   24 to 29   30s   40s   50s   60s   70s   80s

❑ Student/grade _____   ❑ Single   ❑ Solo parent   ❑ Married
❑ Widowed

Do you have children? What are their names and ages?

_____

_____

_____

_____

Tell us about your hobbies, special interests, spiritual gifts, or something about yourself you would like us to know:

_____

_____

_____

Place of employment: _____

Position:_____

Part 2: Your Church Interest and Background

Are you a member of another church? Yes _____ No _____

If yes, which church? _____

Church address: _____

What brought you to Peoples Church? _____

_____

_____

How long have you been attending Peoples Church? _____

Are you attending a Sunday school class? Yes _____ No _____

If so, which one? _____

Please list any ministries of Peoples Church in which you are presently involved: _____

_____

_____

Please list any ministries of Peoples Church in which you have been involved in the past:_____

_____

Please list any organizations outside of Peoples Church you care deeply about and are involved with: _____

_____

Why are you considering membership with Peoples Church?

_____

_____

_____

What would you like to know about Peoples Church?

_____

_____

Part 3: Your Spiritual Journey

Do you believe Jesus Christ to be the Son of God?

Yes _____ No _____

Have you asked Jesus to be your personal Savior?

Yes _____ No _____

Have you been baptized in water?　　　Yes _____ No _____

Have you come to the place in your spiritual life where you know *for certain* that if you were to die today you would go to heaven?

Yes _____ No _____

Suppose you were to die today and stand before God and he were to say to you, "Why should I let you into my heaven?" what would you say? _____

_____

_____

Please share your personal testimony. *As an example you might to tell us what your life was like before you became a Christian, how you became a Christian, and what your life is like now that you are a Christian.* _____

_____

_____

_____

_____

_____

_____

_____

SPIRITUAL QUESTIONNAIRE

adapted from Chapel Hill Presbyterian Church, Gig Harbor,
Washington, and Campus Crusade for Christ International

Spiritual Questionnaire
(to be turned in to your small group leader Friday night)

Name: _____ Date: _____

1. Briefly describe your level of participation in church the last few years.

2. A close friend comes to you and says, "I notice you attend church. I've recently become interested in spiritual things and want to know how I can become a Christian." How would you answer him or her?

3. Suppose something unfortunate happened to you tonight and you died unexpectedly. How certain are you that you would go to heaven?

    _____ Don't know   _____ Hopeful
    _____ Good possibility   _____ Absolutely sure

4. Suppose you died and were standing before God. How would you answer him if he were to ask you, "Why should I let you into my heaven?"

5. *To be answered after the Friday night presentation:* Did the message tonight teach you anything new or help you make any decisions about your faith? Explain.

Sample Gospel Presentation

adapted from "Experiencing God's GRACE" tract
(used by permission)

G . . . stands for GOD

- God is the *beginning* of GRACE. In fact, he is the beginning of all things (Genesis 1:1).
- God, our Creator, is a God of *holiness* and *love*.
- Because God is our loving Creator and Ruler, we are responsible to *love, worship, and obey* him alone (Matthew 22:37–38).

R . . . stands for REBELLION

- Clearly, *all* of us fall short of God's perfect standard (Romans 3:23).
- We are all sinners, both by *nature* and by *choice* (Romans 5:12; 1 John 1:8).
- Our sins have *separated* us from our Creator (Isaiah 59:2).
- Because sin separates us from God, it carries tragic *consequences* (Romans 6:23).

A . . . stands for ATONEMENT

- *Atonement* means "to repair a *broken* relationship." God, because of his great love for his creation, sent his Son—Jesus—into the world so that sinners may be reconciled to God (John 3:16; Romans 5:1).

- By his life, Jesus attained *righteousness* on sinners' behalf. By his death, Jesus paid the *penalty* that sinners owed. By his resurrection, Jesus defeated *death* for all who will follow him.

C . . . stands for CONVERSION

- To receive Jesus as Savior and Lord, we must *trust* in him alone for salvation (John 14:6; Acts 4:12).
- And we must turn from our sins (*repent*) and turn to him in love and obedience (Luke 13:3; John 14:15; Acts 17:30).
- God's GRACE comes to those who *receive* Jesus by faith (John 1:12; Acts 16:31; Romans 1:16; 10:9, 13)

E . . . stands for ETERNAL LIFE

- Jesus brings *new life* to all who place their faith in him (John 10:10; 2 Corinthians 5:17).
- This wonderful *gift* of eternal life is given to all those who have been saved through faith in Jesus.

THE MOST IMPORTANT QUESTION . . .
"Where do I stand in the sight of God?"

- On the cross, Jesus suffered the justice and wrath of God on behalf of all those who trust Jesus as Savior and Lord. On the other hand, those who do not trust Jesus as Savior and Lord will suffer the *judgment* of God themselves (John 3:36).
- There is *no middle ground* with Jesus (Matthew 12:30).

ARE YOU READY?

- If so, then you must *repent* of your sins and place your faith in Jesus alone for salvation. You must *believe* that Jesus lived, died, and rose again for your salvation. You must commit your life to Jesus as your living Savior and Lord. If you are ready to have your sins forgiven and to receive the gift of eternal life, then *trust in Jesus right now*.

LIVING DAILY IN GOD'S GRACE

- *Prayer*. Pray daily.
- *Worship*. Give God the praise he deserves.
- *Bible Study*. Read the Bible daily.
- *Fellowship*. Meet regularly with other Christians who will help you grow in your new life with Jesus Christ.
- *Service*. Serve Jesus and serve your fellow human beings.
- *Witnessing*. Tell others about what Jesus has done in your life.

Appendix 6

SAMPLE LESSON ON THE CHURCH

This class is about church membership, so it's important we understand what *the church* is.

I. PICTURES OF THE CHURCH
    A. The church is called out for a purpose.
    B. The church is a family (2 Corinthians 6:18; Ephesians 3:14; 1 Timothy 5:1–2).
    C. The church is the body of Christ (1 Corinthians 12:1–31).
    D. The church is the bride of Christ (2 Corinthians 11:2; Ephesians 5:32).

II. THE IMPORTANCE OF CHURCH MEMBERSHIP
    A. Biblical evidence
        1. Acts 2:41
        2. Ephesians 5:25
        3. 1 Corinthians 12:27
        4. Hebrews 10:25
        5. 1 Timothy 3:5, Hebrews 13:17
        6. Matthew 18:15–17, 1 Corinthians 5:11–13
    B. Practical arguments
        Church membership:
        1. is a person's public commitment to a particular group of believers.
        2. allows church leaders to fulfill their task of shepherding those who have joined the church.
        3. defines and builds the team that is ready to do the work of the church.

4. offers a support system when believers are tempted or struggling.
5. provides opportunities for spiritual growth under the guidance and accountability of other church members.
6. challenges believers to use their God-given spiritual gifts alongside others God has placed in the church.
7. grants believers permission to offer input and direction for a local church body.
8. provides a family in a rapidly changing society.

III. REQUIREMENTS FOR CHURCH MEMBERSHIP
   A. A salvation experience through Christ
   B. Attendance at the membership class
   C. Baptism

IV. THE ORDINANCES OF THE CHURCH*
   A. Baptism
      1. Jesus commanded it and modeled it (Matthew 28:18–20; Mark 1:9).
      2. Baptism demonstrates belief (Acts 2:41; 18:8).
   B. The Lord's Supper
      1. Jesus commanded it and modeled it (1 Corinthians 11:23–25).
      2. The Lord's Supper demonstrates belief (1 Corinthians 11:26).

*Specific information on these topics vary by denomination. This sample lesson is intended only as a model from which each church can develop its own details.

THE EXPECTATION PENTAGON WORKSHEET

designed to help churches apply this model in their context

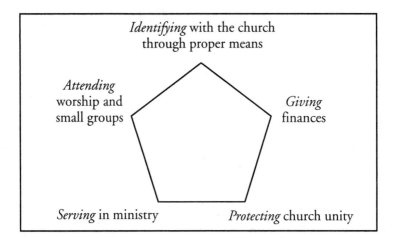

1. *Identifying* with the church through proper means
   Biblical support: Acts 2:41; 18:8; Romans 6:3–4
   Ways to fulfill this commitment in my church:

   _____
   _____
   _____

2. *Attending* worship and small groups
   Biblical support: Psalm 95:6; Acts 2:42; Hebrews 10:25
   Ways to fulfill this commitment in my church:

   _____
   _____
   _____

3. *Giving* finances
   Biblical support: Malachi 3:8–12; 1 Corinthians 16:2;
       2 Corinthians 9:7
   Ways to fulfill this commitment in my church:

   _____

   _____

   _____

4. *Serving* in ministry
   Biblical support: Romans 12:1; 1 Corinthians 12;
       Ephesians 4:11–13
   Ways to fulfill this commitment in my church:

   _____

   _____

   _____

5. *Protecting* church unity
   Biblical support: John 17:11; Acts 1:14; Romans 12:5
   Ways to fulfill this commitment in my church:

   _____

   _____

   _____

SAMPLE MEMBERSHIP COVENANT

adapted from one used by Harpeth Community Church,
Franklin, Tennessee

The leaders of Harpeth Community Church covenant to do their best to be faithful leader-shepherds of Christ in the following ways:

- To hold up Jesus Christ and the core gospel in all things.
- To pray for and seek God's best for the church and all members on a regular basis.
- To devote ourselves to the study, proclamation, and application of God's Word.
- To set a Christlike example for the church in all things.
- To be available for prayer, encouragement, and help when called on by the members.
- To be accountable to the church for our leadership.

The Membership Covenant

- You have personally and consciously repented and placed your faith in Jesus Christ as Savior and Lord and expressed this commitment to trust and follow Jesus in water baptism (immersion).
- You are making a conscious and ongoing commitment to do your best to support the mission, vision, and values of the church—and to signify such by signing the membership covenant:

I will do my best to support the testimony of the gospel and my church family

- by inviting those unconnected with a church to attend (Luke 14:23)
- by looking for ways to share my faith in Jesus Christ with others (Matthew 28:19–20)
- by praying for the church's growth in spirit and numbers (1 Thessalonians 1:1–3)
- by warmly welcoming those who visit church activities (Romans 15:7)

I will do my best to live with devotion for God

- by regular attendance at the Sunday Celebration assemblies (Hebrews 10:23–25)
- by personally trusting and following Jesus Christ as my personal Savior and Lord and by holding to the core of my faith (John 3:16; 2 Corinthians 13:3–5; Galatians 1:6–9)
- by developing a growing personal relationship with God through prayer, Scripture study, and obedience (Psalm 1; 1 Peter 1:13–16)

I will do my best to support and be supported by others in the church

- by regular participation in my small group (Acts 2:42–47)
- by focusing on love as Jesus' central command (John 13:34–35)
- by refusing to gossip or speak ill of others—or even to listen to such things (Ephesians 4:29)
- by seeking reconciliation with other members when conflict or interpersonal problems arise (Matthew 5:21–26; 18:15–20; Ephesians 4:26–27)

I will do my best to grow in Christlikeness

- by picking up my cross and following Jesus in daily life (Mark 8:34–37)
- by studying Scripture (2 Timothy 3:14–4:4)
- by attending church-sponsored seminars (2 Peter 1:5–10)
- by calling my small group leader or one of the church leaders when I need a visit or help (James 5:14–16)
- by living a godly life and being accountable for any serious or ongoing sinful patterns in my life (Matthew 18:15–18; 1 Corinthians 5:9–13; Galatians 6:1–2)

I will do my best to be a minister of Jesus Christ through my church

- by regularly giving back to God a portion of my financial blessings (1 Corinthians 16:2)
- by discovering my gifts and talents and using them in the church (1 Peter 4:10)
- by being equipped by my leaders to serve (Ephesians 4:11–12)
- by developing a servant's heart (Philippians 2:3–4, 7)

MINISTRY OPPORTUNITIES CHECKLIST

Name: _____

Phone: _____

Email: _____

Please mark the following areas where you may be interested in serving. Return your form to the collection box in the welcome center.

SUNDAY SCHOOL:
_____ Sunday school director
_____ Sunday school secretary
_____ Nursery teacher
_____ Preschool teacher
_____ Children's teacher
_____ Youth teacher
_____ Adult teacher
_____ Classroom assistant
      Age/group: _____
_____ Substitute teacher
      Age/group: _____

NURSERY/EXTENDED SESSION/CHILDREN'S CHURCH:
_____ Nursery worker as needed
    _____ Sunday a.m.
    _____ Sunday p.m.
    _____ Wednesday p.m.

_____ Extended session worker
      (K–5 yrs) as needed
_____ Children's Church worker as needed
_____ Musician for Children's Church

MUSIC PROGRAM:
_____ Adult choir member
_____ Instrumentalist:
      _____
_____ Youth choir leader
_____ Youth choir assistant
_____ Children's choir leader
_____ Children's choir assistant
_____ Preschool choir leader
_____ Preschool choir assistant
_____ Drama participant (actor)
_____ Drama leader (director/writer)

____ Soloist
____ Sound crew
____ Lighting crew

MEN'S MINISTRY:
____ Leader
____ Participant

WOMEN'S MINISTRY:
____ Leader
____ Participant

MISSIONS MINISTRIES:
____ Children's missions leader
____ Children's missions assistant
____ Preschool missions leader
____ Preschool missions assistant
____ Mission trip leader
____ Mission trip participant
____ Women's missions leader
____ Women's missions participant
____ Men's missions leader
____ Men's missions participant
____ Church minister of missions

MAINTENANCE:
____ Building maintenance help
____ Building cleaning help
____ Parking lot maintenance
____ Lawn care help

OUTREACH:
____ Visitation/outreach
____ Hospital visitation
____ Telephone calls
____ Note writing to guests
____ Food preparation
____ Shut-in visitation
____ Usher
____ Auto repair
____ Van driver
____ Deaf ministry
____ Mentoring new believers
____ Evangelistic counseling
____ Senior adult ministry
____ Puppet ministry
____ New members ministry
____ Kitchen committee
____ Public relations committee
____ Resource room coordinator
____ Crafts ministry
____ Donut ministry director
____ Divorce care ministry
____ Single adult ministry
____ Prayer ministry
____ Youth ministry

ADMINISTRATIVE/OFFICE HELP:
____ Computer support
____ Clerical help
____ Newsletter preparation
____ Volunteer receptionist

"DISCOVERING YOUR MINISTRY" WORKSHEET

adapted from the one used by Johnson Ferry Baptist Church, Marietta, Georgia

I. EXAMINE YOUR PAST (ACTS 22:1–21)

    A. *Family Background*: What are some characteristics of your family and upbringing that might identify the types of people, needs, or ministry God is calling you to address? (e.g., suburban family, military background, blended family)

        1. _____

        2. _____

    B. *Career Experiences*: What skills or interests do you believe God may have been developing as a result of your career history? (e.g., sales/people skills, management/administration)

        1. _____

        2. _____

    C. *Spiritual Training Points*: What are some key experiences God has used to shape your major life decisions and to teach you spiritual lessons? (e.g., survived cancer/empathy toward the sick, job loss/God will provide)

        1. _____

        2. _____

II. Examine Your Heart (Nehemiah 1:1–12)

    A. *Personal Compassion*: For which groups of people or special needs has God placed a strong sense of compassion in your heart? (e.g., homeless, single parents, new believers)

        1. _____

        2. _____

    B. *Personal Fulfillment*: Which activities, hobbies, or interests would you love for God to use as a platform for ministry in your life? (e.g., skiing, lake house, sports)

        1. _____

        2. _____

III. Examine Your Vision (Acts 2:17–18)

    A. *Ministry Ideas*: What ideas for ministry has God repeatedly and persistently brought to your attention with a sense of interest and excitement? (e.g., rest home ministry, disabilities ministry, mentoring young professionals)

        1. _____

        2. _____

    B. *God's Activity*: Among which group of people, in what service or ministry, do you personally and clearly see God powerfully at work? (e.g., homemakers in the neighborhood, unemployed support groups)

        1. _____

        2. _____

IV. SUMMARY

Reflecting on your past, your heart, and your vision, list a few ministry directions you will prayerfully investigate to see whether God is inviting you there for ministry.

1. _____

2. _____

3. _____

4. _____

Sample Sermon Outline

Bible Reading: 1 Corinthians 12

I want you to think today about gifts—about presents you have received. Sometimes we get gifts we really don't need, but they're just fun (like the battery-operated airplane I received when I was twenty years old). At other times we get gifts we didn't ask for, but somebody else knew we needed (like the toolbox and tools I received when I really wanted a set of golf clubs!). In either case, the gift is good for us.

God, too, gives us gifts—spiritual gifts—that are good for us. We may not always recognize our need for them, and we don't always realize how important they are as we serve in the church. But I hope today you can begin to see how God wants to use your gifts in the church.

I. DISCOVERING AND USING YOUR GIFTS IS FOR THE GOOD OF THE CHURCH

> The Spirit gives gifts to all believers (verses 6–7), and he gives us those gifts for the common good. He gives gifts according to his will (verse 11), knowing what is best for the church. He arranges the body in such a way that our diversity of gifts contributes to his plan; we march together, even though we are differently gifted. When each person in the church uses these gifts, the church is that much stronger.

II. Using Our Gifts Helps Us Realize Our Significance in the Church

> Some in the church in Corinth were battling over who had the best gifts (verses 14–26). Some felt less significant, less important to the body. Paul reminded them that God put the body together as he wished, giving honor even to the weaker parts. To those in the church who feel they have nothing to offer, Paul says, "You, too, are important to the body. Use your gifts." It's our job as church leaders and members to help all of our members find their place of ministry.

III. Using Our Gifts Helps Us Find Joy

> Each one of us is a part of God's body (verse 27). God has arranged his body so that each of us has a unique place in it (verse 18). He chooses to use each of us for the common good (verse 7). What more exciting place can there be than to be right where God wants us to be, to be doing exactly what he wants us to do? There is joy in that kind of obedience.

If you are not currently serving in this church—that is, if you're not using your God-given gifts to the fullest—we want to help you. We are committed to leading our members to do ministry. You make the commitment, and we'll walk you through the process.

New Member Evaluation Form

adapted from the one used by Carlisle Baptist Church,
Panama City, Florida

Questionnaire

I. AWARENESS

A. How did you learn about _____ Church?

_____ phone book _____ signs _____ Internet
_____ other advertisement
_____ personal invitation by:
_____ friend _____ lay member _____ minister
_____ other: _____

B. What was happening in your life when you came to
_____ Church?

_____ geographical move _____ marriage
_____ divorce   _____ birth of a child
_____ financial crisis   _____ spiritual crisis
_____ health crisis   _____ death of significant
                               other in your life
_____ other: _____
_____ none of the above

C. What were you looking for in a church family? _____
_____

D. What originally attracted you to this church? _____
   _____
   _____

E. When you first attended, were you identified and welcomed as a guest? _____ Yes _____ No
   If so, how? _____
   _____

F. Was there anything that almost kept you from becoming active in this congregation? _____ Yes _____ No
   If so, what was it? _____

G. How much time passed between the time you started attending and the time you decided to join?
   ____ fewer than 2 weeks ____ several weeks to 3 months
   ____ 3 to 6 months   ____ 6 to 12 months
   ____ more than a year

II. Hospitality

A. Did a layperson or team visit or call you after you began attending? _____ Yes _____ No
   If so, how long after your first visit were you contacted?
   _____

B. Did a minister visit or call you? _____ Yes _____ No
   If so, how long after your first visit were you contacted?
   _____

C. When did you feel accepted in this congregation?
   _____ after my first visit
   _____ after attending a small group
   _____ when I joined
   _____ after attending the membership class
   _____ I still don't feel accepted

D. What, if any, surprises did you experience while getting acquainted with this congregation?

    _____

    _____

    _____

E. Has any experience with this church made you feel uncomfortable, awkward, or "put off"?

    _____ Yes _____ No

    If so, what happened? _____

    _____

F. Describe the most moving or satisfying personal experience you've had in this church.

    _____

    _____

    _____

III. RESPONSE

A. Besides Sunday worship, in which church programs or activities did you first become active?

    _____

    _____

    _____

B. How did you get involved in your first activity?

    _____ personal initiative

    _____ response to a pulpit or bulletin announcement

    _____ response to a personal invitation from a church member or staff

    _____ other: _____

C. Who most helped you move deeper into the life of the church? If possible, provide names or positions.

    _____

    _____

D. Does our church do a good job of making its ministries and programs known to new members?
_____ Yes _____ No

E. Which programs or ministries do you wish you knew more about or had known about sooner?

_____

_____

_____

F. Have you been made aware of members' financial responsibilities? _____ Yes _____ No

G. Has the congregation communicated to you what it expects of its members? _____ Yes _____ No

H. Briefly describe what you understand to be the church's major expectations.

_____

_____

_____

IV. GOING DEEPER

A. As you evaluate a church, how important is the Sunday worship experience?

Unimportant   Very important
1   2   3   4   5   6   7   8

B. Rate _____ Church in its ability to meet your worship needs.

Unable   Very able
1   2   3   4   5   6   7   8

C. Did the church encourage you as a new member to develop personal spiritual disciplines?
_____ Yes _____ No

D. Have you noticed any intentional church efforts to help newcomers and long-term members get to know each other better? _____ Yes _____ No

V. MEMBERSHIP CLASS

A. Please rate the overall value of the membership class.

Not valuable   Very valuable

1   2   3   4   5   6   7   8

B. Which lessons or topics were most valuable to you?

_____

_____

_____

C. Which lessons or topics were least valuable to you?

_____

_____

_____

D. What changes would you suggest?

_____

_____

_____

Name: _____ Phone: _____

Email: _____

SPIRITUAL GROWTH CHECKLIST

Name: _____ Phone: _____

Address: _____

_____

Email: _____

GENERAL AREA: **SPECIFIC TOPICS:**

Knowledge

Basic Bible organization and knowledge

Plan of salvation

Basic church doctrine/structure

Denominational structure/polity

Other: _____

_____

Courses taken	Date	Conferences attended	Date	Books read	Date	Meetings with mentor
New Testament	5/04	Evangelism Explosion training	1/03	*Systematic Theology*	1/04	

CHURCH SURVEY

New Member Class Survey
Billy Graham School of Missions, Evangelism and Church Growth

I. Basic Church Information

Church name: _____

Street address: _____

_____

City: _____ State: _____ Zip: _____

Phone: (day) (___) _____ (evening) (___) _____

Fax (if applicable): (___) _____

Email: _____

Age of the church (number of years the church has been in existence as a constituted body): _____ years _____ months

Name of person completing this survey: _____

_____

Position held in the church: _____

Phone (if needed to clarify responses) : (____)_____

Email: _____

Does your church currently have a new member class:

_____ Yes _____ No

If your response to the previous question is "no," complete only sections I and II, and then return the survey to the Graham School. All others should respond to the rest of the survey.

A. Please use the information from your annual church profile (SBC) or your church minutes to complete the following information. If your church does not keep records for the following categories, please mark N/A.

1. Resident membership _____
2. Average morning worship attendance _____
3. Average Sunday school/cell group attendance _____
4. Total additions by conversion (baptism) _____
5. Total additions by transfer of membership _____
6. Total of *ALL* additions _____

B. Please provide the following geographic and demographic information about the church.

7. Church setting:

_____ a. Open country/rural area

_____ b. Town (500 to 2,499 people)

_____ c. Small city (2,500 to 9,999 people)

_____ d. Medium city/downtown (10,000 to 49,999 people)

_____ e. Medium city/suburbs (10,000 to 49,999 people)

_____ f. Large city/downtown or inner city (50,000+ people)

_____ g. Large city/suburbs (50,000+ people)

8. Congregational demographics of *active* membership

Race		Age		Economic Levels	
Caucasian	_____%	under 18	_____%	Upper class	_____%
African-American	_____%	19–35	_____%	Middle class	_____%
		36–50	_____%	Lower class	_____%
Hispanic	_____%	51–65	_____%		
Asian	_____%	66+	_____%		
Other:	_____%				

II. Church Staff Information

9. Senior pastor's name: _____

10. Senior pastor's highest education level:
    _____ a. High school _____ c. Seminary (master's degree)
    _____ b. College _____ d. Seminary (doctorate)
    _____ e. Seminary studies (no degree)

11. Is the senior pastor full-time? _____ Yes _____ No

12. How long has the senior pastor served at the church?
    _____ years _____ months

13. Which other paid staff positions does the church have?
    _____ a. associate pastor
    _____ b. minister of music/worship
    _____ c. minister of education
    _____ d. minister of youth/students
    _____ e. others

III. New Member Class Information

14. How long has the church had a new member class?
    _____ years _____ months

15. Please list any obstacles the church faced in establishing a new member class (e.g., opposition from leaders, questions about who should attend)

    _____

    _____

    _____

16. Does your church require or expect new members to attend a new member course?
    _____ Require _____ Expect _____ Neither

17. What does your church call the new member class (what name do you use for the course)? _____

    _____

18. If you require a new member class, must the course be completed *before* new members are accepted by vote into the church? ____Yes ____No ____N/A

19. Are prospects and visitors permitted and/or encouraged to attend the new member/orientation course?
    _____ Permitted _____ Encouraged
    _____ Neither (class is reserved for new members)

20. Using the following scale, indicate the purpose(s) of your new member class.

1	2	3	4	5
Not at all a purpose		Somewhat a purpose		A primary purpose

    _____ a. providing orientation to the church in general
    _____ b. teaching about the church's basic doctrine
    _____ c. building relationships among new members
    _____ d. introducing class members to the church staff
    _____ e. offering opportunities for new members to get involved in the ministry of the church
    _____ f. carrying out evangelism—sharing the gospel with class members
    _____ g. other: _____

21. Who teaches the new member class?
    _____ a. Senior pastor _____ c. Layperson
    _____ b. Staff member _____ d. Other

22. When does the new member course meet?
    Day(s): _____ Time: _____ # of sessions: _____

23. How often is the course offered? _____

24. Does the class meet ____ on campus or ____ off campus?

25. Which of the following topics are addressed in the new member class? Please mark all that apply.

_____ a. Doctrine of the church
_____ b. Polity and government of your church
_____ c. History of your church
_____ d. Requirements for membership
_____ e. Expectations of members after joining
_____ f. Policies for disciplining/excluding members
_____ g. Training for witnessing/evangelism
_____ h. Training in spiritual disciplines (prayer, study, etc.)
_____ i. Plan of salvation
_____ j. Examination of the church covenant
_____ k. Inventory of spiritual gifts
_____ l. Explanation of the church's mission and/or vision
_____ m. Structure, history, and polity of the denomination
_____ n. Introductions to church staff and leadership
_____ o. Current opportunities for service in the church
_____ p. Tithing/financial support of the church
_____ q. Examination of the church constitution
_____ r. Structure/support of missions through the Cooperative Program (SBC) or other denominational programs
_____ s. Method and meaning of baptism
_____ t. Purpose of the Lord's Supper
_____ u. Tour of the church facilities
_____ v. Other: _____

26. If your church uses a specific book, study guide, or kit for the new member class, what resource(s) do you use? Please be specific. If you have produced your own materials, would you please send us a copy?

_____

_____

_____

27. Do you have an established means by which you evaluate the new member class? _____ Yes _____ No _____ N/A

28. If you do evaluate the class, how do you do so?

_____

_____

29. What percentage of members who have joined within the past two years attended a new member class? _____%

30. What percentage of members who have joined within the last two years are currently active in the church (attending worship at least twice a month and involved in some other type of activity or ministry in the church)? _____%

31. What percentage of your current active members have completed a new member class at your church? _____%

32. What ONE change would you like to see made in the church's new member class? _____

_____

33. Many church leaders ask the question, "If we begin a new member class, should the long-term members be expected or required to take it?" How does your church address this important question?

_____

_____

34. Using the following scale, respond to each of the statements below:

1	2	3	4	5
Strongly disagree	Disagree	Uncertain	Agree	Strongly agree

_____ a. A new member class should be required before joining a church.

_____ b. A new member class is too much work to make it worthwhile.

_____ c. Our church is a stronger church because we have a new member class.

_____ d. The pastor should be the primary teacher of a new member class.

_____ e. The new member class should be no longer than one session.

35. How can we at the Billy Graham School best help you strengthen your new member class? What other information would you like that might help you?

_____

_____

_____

Please include with your responses any outlines, curriculum, materials, etc., you use that may help us better understand your church's new member class.

Return this survey, the two members' surveys, and any other information to the Graham School, using the envelope provided. Thank you for your help with this important study.

New Member Survey

New Member Class Survey
Billy Graham School of Missions, Evangelism and Church Growth

Church name: _____

Street address: _____

City: _____ State: _____ Zip: _____

Your name: _____

Street address: _____

_____

City: _____ State: _____ Zip: _____

Phone: (day) (___) _____ (evening) (___) _____

Email: _____

1. How long had you been a Christian when you attended your church's new member class? _____

2. Did your church *require* you to attend this class? _____ Yes _____ No

3. If your church required you to attend, are you now glad you attended the class? _____ Yes _____ No _____ N/A

4. Using this scale, indicate how your participation in a new member class influenced your life.

1	2	3	4	5	6	7	8	9	10

Strongly disagree	Disagree	Uncertain	Agree	Strongly agree

_____ a. I know more about my church now.

_____ b. I know more about studying the Bible now.

_____ c. I know more people in the church now.

_____ d. I am more prepared to tell others about Jesus now.

_____ e. I would be more comfortable talking to my pastor now.

_____ f. I pray more often now.

_____ g. I understand more about baptism and the Lord's Supper now.

_____ h. I am now more willing to give financially to my church.

_____ i. I know more about my denomination now (if applicable).

_____ j. I am now more willing to get involved in the church by leading or supporting a ministry of the church.

_____ k. I now know the church's expectations for its members.

_____ l. I understand now the church's policy for discipline of its members.

_____ m. I now know my spiritual gift(s).

_____ n. I know more about God now.

_____ o. I am more willing to invite friends to church now.

5. What were the primary benefits you received from attending your church's new member class?

_____

_____

_____

6. What would you like to see changed about the new member class? What improvements could be made?

_____

_____

_____

7. Would you recommend that this class be *required* for all new members? Why or why not?

_____

_____

_____

CHURCHES THAT PARTICIPATED IN THIS STUDY

First Baptist Church
Winthrop Harbor, Illinois

Temple Hill Baptist Church
Granite Falls, North Carolina

North Fork Baptist Church
Eufaula, Oklahoma

Mountain Grove Baptist Church
Granite Falls, North Carolina

Calvary Baptist Church
Ruston, Louisiana

Lakeside Baptist Church
Greensboro, Georgia

Oak Hill Baptist Church
Griffin, Georgia

First Baptist Church
Neosho, Missouri

Cross Roads Baptist Church
Fort Myers, Florida

Trinity Baptist Church
Weatherford, Oklahoma

First Baptist Church
Perry, Oklahoma

Johnson Ferry Baptist Church
Marietta, Georgia

First Baptist Church
Umatilla, Florida

Bethany Baptist Church
Andalusia, Alabama

Edgewood Baptist Center &
Chapel
Dayton, Ohio

Piner Baptist Church
Morning View, Kentucky

Southeast Baptist Church
Owensboro, Kentucky

Englewood Baptist Church
Jackson, Tennessee

Trinity Baptist Church
Benton, Arkansas

New Prospect Baptist Church
Lawrenceburg, Tennessee

Northside Baptist Church
Tifton, Georgia

First Baptist Church
Marietta, Oklahoma

First Baptist Church
Okay, Oklahoma

Moss Bluff Baptist Church
Ocklawaha, Florida

Union Grove Baptist Church
Beech Bluff, Tennessee

First Baptist Church
Panama City, Florida

Orlinda Baptist Church
Orlinda, Tennessee

Friendship Baptist Church
Beaumont, Texas

Greenwell Springs Baptist Church
Greenwell Springs, Louisiana

Rose Drive Baptist Church
Yorba Linda, California

Union Baptist Church
Union, Kentucky

Center Hill Baptist Church
Loganville, Georgia

Faith Evangelical Free Church
Woodruff, Wisconsin

Pine Level Baptist Church
Early Branch, South Carolina

Cedar Street Church
Holt, Michigan

Wakulla Springs Baptist Church
Crawfordville, Florida

Valley View Church
Louisville, Kentucky

First Baptist Church
Belleview, Florida

Harpeth Community Church
Franklin, Tennessee

Carlisle Baptist Church
Panama City, Florida

Hunter Street Baptist Church
Birmingham, Alabama

Mountain View Presbyterian
Church
Scottsdale, Arizona

Mililani Baptist Church
Mililani, Hawaii

Lebanon Evangelical Free Church
Lebanon, Ohio

First Baptist Church
Anchorage, Alaska

First Baptist Church
Aurora, Missouri

East Booneville Baptist Church
Booneville, Mississippi

Chapel Hill Presbyterian Church
Gig Harbor, Washington

Countryside Baptist Church
Clearwater, Florida

Lakota Hills Baptist Church
West Chester, Ohio

Red Mountain Baptist Church
Rougemont, North Carolina

First Baptist Church
Pembroke, Georgia

Cresthill Baptist Church
Bowie, Maryland

First Baptist Church
Naples, Florida

West Main Baptist Church
Artesia, New Mexico

New Life Presbyterian Church
Fruitland Park, Florida

Stonegate Fellowship
Midland, Texas

First Evangelical Free Church
Ames, Iowa

Cottonwood Church
Albuquerque, New Mexico

Braelinn Church
Peachtree City, Georgia

Advent Presbyterian Church
Cordova, Tennessee

Peoples Church
Fresno, California

Lutheran Church of the Redeemer
Birmingham, Michigan

Manchester Christian Church
Manchester, New Hampshire

Woodlawn Baptist Church
Hopewell, Virginia

Westside Baptist Church
Sapulpa, Oklahoma

Oak Grove Baptist Church
Hugo, Oklahoma

Sarasota Baptist Church
Sarasota, Florida

Ingleside Baptist Church
Macon, Georgia

Carpenter's Way Baptist Church
Lufkin, Texas

Coastal Community Church
Virginia Beach, Virginia

Hayward Wesleyan Church
Hayward, Wisconsin

Sandia Presbyterian Church
Albuquerque, New Mexico

First Southern Baptist Church
Salina, Kansas

Centerview Baptist Church
Jacksonville, North Carolina

Peninsula Baptist Church
Mooresville, North Carolina

North Lanier Church
Cumming, Georgia

Deep Creek Baptist Church
Chesapeake, Virginia

Hillcrest Baptist Church
Lebanon, Tennessee

South Biscayne Baptist Church
North Port, Florida

Pine First Baptist Church
Franklinton, Louisiana

The Church at Crossgate Center
Hot Springs, Arkansas

Union Hill Baptist Church
Oneonta, Alabama

Mt. Pleasant Baptist Church
Carrollton, Georgia

The Country Church
Marion, Texas

Petsworth Baptist Church
Gloucester, Virginia

Cornerstone Baptist Church
Harker Heights, Texas

NOTES

1. See Thom Rainer, *Effective Evangelistic Churches* (Nashville: Broadman and Holman, 1996), 178–79; Rainer, *High Expectations* (Nashville: Broadman and Holman, 1999), 103–19.

2. See Rainer, *High Expectations*, 104.

3. Chuck Lawless, *Discipled Warriors: Growing Healthy Churches That Are Equipped for Spiritual Warfare* (Grand Rapids: Kregel, 2002).

4. See Rainer, *High Expectations*, 103–19.

5. See Barna Research Group, "Born Again Christians," research archives; can be viewed on the Web at www.barna.org/FlexPage.aspx?Page=Topic&TopicID=8.

6. William Langford, "Designing a Program That Develops Attenders into Ministers at the Lakota Hills Baptist Church, West Chester, Ohio" (D.Min. project, The Southern Baptist Theological Seminary, 1999), 108.

7. Langford, "Designing a Program," 103–4.

8. See Charles Arn, "How to Assimilate Newcomers into Your Church"; can be viewed on the Web at www.netresults.org/workshops/arn.htm.

9. See Lyle E. Schaller, *Assimilating New Members* (Nashville: Abingdon, 1978), 74; Elmer L. Towns, "Evangelism: The Why and How," in *Church Growth: State of the Art*, C. Peter Wagner, ed. (Wheaton, Ill.: Tyndale House, 1988), 53; Win Arn and Charles Arn, *The Master's Plan for Making Disciples* (Grand Rapids: Baker, 1998), 45–46.

10. See Rainer, *High Expectations*, 11–28; Rainer, *Surprising Insights from the Unchurched and Proven Ways to Reach Them* (Grand Rapids: Zondervan, 2001), 107–24.

11. Calvin Ratz, "The Velcro Church," *Leadership* 11 (Fall 1990): 38.

12. See Rainer, *Surprising Insights*, 187–207. Rainer notes that pastors of growing churches tend to be more task driven and less relationally oriented.

13. See Rainer, *High Expectations*, 104–9.

14. See Rainer, *Surprising Insights*, 149.

15. Taken from *The Purpose-Driven® Church* by RICK WARREN. Copyright © 1995 by Rick Warren. Used by permission of The Zondervan Corporation.

16. Rick Warren, *The Purpose-Driven Church* (Grand Rapids: Zondervan, 1995), 145.

17. Warren, *The Purpose-Driven Church*, 315, 317.

18. Warren, *The Purpose-Driven Church*, 318.

19. See Ralph O. Burns, *Basic Bible Truths* (Schaumburg, Ill.: Regular Baptist Press, 1971).

20. See *Welcome to the Family!* (Minneapolis: Evangelical Free Church of America, 2000).

21. We recommend the *Experiencing God's GRACE* tract; can be viewed on the Web at www.sbts.edu/academics/GRACE.pdf. To obtain a copy, contact the Southern Seminary Lifeway campus store at 502-897-4056.

22. See Warren, *The Purpose-Driven Church*, 86–94; Henry Klopp, *The Ministry Playbook* (Grand Rapids: Baker, 2002), 163–67; George Hunter, *Leading and Managing a Growing Church* (Nashville: Abingdon, 2000), 62–65.

23. Hunter, *Leading and Managing*, 63.

24. See Warren, *The Purpose-Driven Church*, 169–72.

25. See Kevin Hamm, "Growing Your Church," *LeaderLife* 2 (Fall 2004): 55.

26. Bruce Bugbee, *Network Revised: The Right People, in the Right Places, for the Right Reasons, at the Right Time* (Grand Rapids: Zondervan, 2005).

27. For more information, visit www.churchgrowth.org/cgi-cg/gifts.cgi.

28. For more information, visit http://mintools.com/spiritual-gifts-test.htm.

29. C. Peter Wagner, *Finding Your Spiritual Gifts: Wagner-Modified Houts Questionnaire* (Ventura, Calif.: Regal, 1995); can be viewed on the Web at www.agts.edu/community/wagner_modified_houts.pdf.

30. John S. Powers, *The BodyLife Journey: Guiding Believers into Ministry* (Nashville: Lifeway, 2001), 10–16.

31. Warren, *The Purpose-Driven Church*, 321–22.

32. Cited in Michael Marot, "Colts Will Open Camp with High Expectations," *Louisville Courier-Journal* (August 1, 2004), C10.

33. See Cynthia Woolever and Deborah Bruce, *A Field Guide to U.S. Congregations* (Louisville, Ky.: Westminster John Knox, 2002), 38.

34. See Robert C. Fuller, *Spiritual but Not Religious: Understanding Unchurched America* (New York: Oxford Univ. Press, 2001), 3.

35. See Jason P. Schachter, "Current Population Reports" (March 2004); can be viewed on the Web at www.census.gov/prod/2004pubs/p20-549.pdf.

36. Reported in Leslie Scanlon, "'Friends' Find a Church, Participate, But Refuse Joining," *Religion News Service* (July 21, 2003).

37. Bob Russell, *When God Builds a Church* (West Monroe, La: Howard, 2000), 113.

38. Russell, *When God Builds a Church*, 119–20.

39. Cited in Jerry W. McCant, *The Meaning of Church Membership* (Kansas City, Mo.: Beacon Hill, 1973), 31–32.

40. An Internet search for "DISC profile" will provide information on training to utilize this resource (for example, see www.DiscProfile.com). This profile is included as part of the *BodyLife Journey* materials.

41. See Warren, *The Purpose-Driven Church*, 369–75; Wayne Cordeiro, *Doing Church as a Team* (Ventura, Calif.: Regal, 2001), 67–72; John Powers, *BodyLife Journey* (Nashville: Lifeway, 2001), 4.

42. See Win Arn, *The Church Growth Ratio Book* (Pasadena, Calif.: Church Growth, Inc., 1987), 10.

43. Robert Dale, *Pastoral Leadership* (Nashville: Abingdon, 1986), 154.

44. Sharon Ellard, "Value-Based Affirmation," can be viewed on the Web at http://sundayschool.ag.org/02Administration/a_tapr_0302valuebased.cfm.

45. Steve Sjogren, *The Perfectly Imperfect Church* (Loveland, Colo.: Group, 2002), 31.

46. See Langford, "Designing a Program," 113–18.

47. Craig L. Blomberg, *Matthew* (New American Commentary 22; Nashville: Broadman and Holman, 1992), 167. Blomberg quotes F. D. Bruner (*The Christbook* [Waco, Tex.: Word, 1987], 366).

48. See Barna Research Group, "Born Again Christians," on the Web at www.barna.org/FlexPage.aspx?Page=Topic&TopicID=8.

49. See Thom S. Rainer, *The Bridger Generation* (Nashville: Broadman and Holman, 1997), 166.

50. See Ralph Neighbour, *Survival Kit for New Christians: Children's Edition* (Nashville: Lifeway, 1981); Todd Capps and Sherry Shaw, *I'm a Christian Now!* (Nashville: Lifeway, 2003).

51. No reader will agree with everything these churches are doing and teaching. The goal of this chapter is simply to introduce you to their specific membership and ministry placement strategies.

52. The seven core commitments are (1) worship as often as possible; (2) invite unchurched neighbors, friends, and relatives to services and activities; (3) give financially to help support the work of Jesus Christ in and through Sandia Presbyterian Church; (4) participate in one or more small groups; (5) find your ministry; (6) engage in personal devotions; and (7) be in the best SHAPE you can be.

53. See Lawless, *Discipled Warriors*, 43.

54. Chuck Lawless, *Making Disciples through Mentoring* (Lynchburg, Va.: Church Growth Institute, 2002).

Subject Index

We want to hear from you. Please send your comments about this book to us in care of zreview@zondervan.com. Thank you.

ZONDERVAN.com/
AUTHORTRACKER
follow your favorite authors